Common Ground

Common Ground

Musings of Mind and Spirit

J. MICHAELS

RESOURCE *Publications* · Eugene, Oregon

COMMON GROUND
Musings of Mind and Spirit

Resource Publications
An Imprint of Wipf and Stock Publishers
199 W. 8th Ave., Suite 3
Eugene, OR 97401
www.wipfandstock.com

ISBN 13: 978-1-49825-485-4

Manufactured in the U.S.A.

To all good souls yearning for Home

Contents

Preface

THIS WAS MY FIRST book of poems. It is the book that started me down a new and exciting path in my life. The first poem you will read is about the brothers Nicobod and Icobod or as I like to call them, the boys of similar name. The brothers appeared to me in a dream in the summer of 2008 and from there, my life changed. As I started to record the poems that came to me on an increasingly frequent and insistent basis, I realized that something deep within had indeed changed. I had made a connection; one I had hoped for and dreamed of for many years.

The poems did not emanate from a voice or a vision. They were not told to me as parable or narrative. Simply put, I had discovered a place where a greater mind than my everyday rational mind lived. And now, on these poetic occasions, I could travel there and bring back these wonderful pearls I have come to love and treasure so much.

I have written over four hundred poems since that first restless night in 2008. And yet not a single one has been planned, constructed, or composed. They were all simply known and delivered. To this day, they continue to come in the same manner. First a word, a title, or a line pops into my head. This is followed immediately by a knowing that I am to write it down. I write that first word or line and the story unfolds from there. At the beginning, I have no idea whatsoever what the poem will be or how it will be written. I simply start writing and as the words appear on the paper, I am always surprised by what comes from my pen. The ode ends when it is supposed to, and again, it is something that is just known. After the poem is completed, I go back and read it. And each and every time, I am amazed by what I have written. Each one is as much a surprise to me as it will be to you when you read it for the first time.

A friend recently asked me if I still read a lot and it gave me pause. After some thought, I realized that I did still read a lot, albeit only from A Course in Miracles and my own books. Since the poems began, I have become more interested in poetry in general but still have not found any

I like as much as the words that are delivered through me. I believe they are gifts, as much for me as for everyone else who is destined to read them. Actually, it works out quite well as I am able to make minor adjustments as I read them for my own pleasure. Generally, they require minimal editing but I do come across some that I obviously did not scribe correctly. I will eventually receive the correct word or phrase in the same manner as the original and that same knowing will verify the change for me. When the editing process is complete, I feel like I have delivered a baby. All I want to do is hold it, look at it, and love it. It may seem silly to you, especially considering my gender, but they truly feel like my children. I then hand them over to my most excellent publisher, who handles them with the same care, and they are eventually delivered to you, the reader.

I believe there are no accidents. I believe the people that we each need in our lives, both to teach and learn from, come to us via the mysterious workings of the Holy Spirit of God. If you are holding this book in your hand and it touches something inside you, you are one of those people. When I read the poems I convey, I feel exactly the same way.

This simple book of verse seems to contain a greater number of stories than the others I have written so far. There is something about learning from a story that is special. It paints a picture and invites us to enter by way of that image. I love the stories presented here; the tale of the gentle giant stolen from his home in Africa and sold into slavery, the first mate who is unable to raise his captain during a fierce storm at sea, or the rebel soldier who lies dieing on the battlefield. All of these convey a spiritual message; be it forgiveness, putting our faith in the right place, or leaving the world for a better place. They are interwoven with other fables, insights, humorous tales, and prayers. They all come from a place where we live; a place with no address, a place where we hold no bed, a place that lives only in ancient memory, but nevertheless, our home. And if we go deep enough, each of us will eventually find that place that we hunger for without knowing why or when or where. My hope and prayer is that somewhere in these pages, that ancient memory will be touched and the aide memoire we all wait for will reach out and touch your heart. If so, I will be a happy man and will consider my time well-spent.

Nicobod & Icobod

Nicobod and Icobod went up the hill
Through the valley and round the bend
They went high and they went low
They went to and they went fro
From here to there they went
Looking up and fell down
Looking for good and evil found
Searching for truth, looking for peace
Til they came upon a stone
A large obstacle in their way
They pushed and shoved
They pulled and prodded
But the stone remained
And ever will, until they know
Where lives the stone
And its refrain

Rick Sheetz

I saw Rick Sheetz last night
A foe from years gone by
A minor adversary once
Now a shadow of unforgiveness

We battled briefly, Rick and I
Both taking positions opposed
Squaring off over meaningless matters
That somehow seemed worthy of foes

But time does heal some wounds
And dims the importance of others
Life and lessons learned
Causes blades to lower, shields to fall

He came to me in a dream
A specter from a prior delusion
The past so unimportant now
Forgiven by me, at least
Brothers in spirit released

Lucky You, Ego Me

You are weak and I am strong
I am right and you are wrong
I see clearly and you do not
Measly is your lot
My way is surely the way to go
You move too awkwardly, you move too slow
Come with me and follow my lead
I must be right, I am your need
Some day you will thank me
Some day you will see
That had you not found me
Where on earth would you be

Great Gifts

True gifts beget not money, success, or fame
Nor emanate from work or academics
Neither are they purchased or lent
Nor offered by merchant's wares
Great gifts come from the heart
Borne of the love bequeathed
They are the invisible offerings
That fashion us strong and well-made
So look not to possessions to make you happy
For they cannot and never will
But pay heed as you chase them
For chase them you likely will
But never forget what helped to mold you
And never forget whose love forged you
For the Father who calls you Son
Is the greatest gift you will ever own

Quantum Love

Science at last has pierced the veil
Parted eons ago by love
The truth of oneness finally revealed
To the eye of the misanthropist

Beyond the microscope and telescope too
Yet close enough to be among us
Exceeding sight, sound, and touch
Yet lying within the fabric
Of universe mechanics exposed

The scientific eye, blind until now
Opened at last by love's experiment
Bringing the last of Spirit's foes
To the truth of Oneness

The skeptic now turns away
From separation's steely glance
Allowing mind to accept what is real
Now it is named and proven true
The Oneness called Love
That has always been

A Man of Unlikely Means

Here I am, a man of unlikely means
Graying now, an older being
Contradictions aplenty, differences abound
Streetwise, yet tempered by love

Years spent in battle and strife
Enemies made but brothers too
A peaceful man, arrived from rage
A lover of God, past hate and solitude

A loner to be sure, feeling safe only inside
Wary of the world and its inhabitants
Remaining in the brain box for so long
Peeking out only to view the boundaries

A lover of thought but rarely shared
A priest but never vowed
In need of love and brothers
Never revealed until now

The Door

Truth no longer hidden
Now revealed and shared
I know nothing and know it

With Christ as my guide
And my brother by my side
I pray I may show it

From all to nothing, back to all
Discard the world's knowledge
Receive the divine sounding

It waits but for the knocking
The door remains unlocked
Simply turn the handle, my brother
And become what you thought not

Love Thought Lost

I dreamed my arrogance cost me love
My imperfection denied it too
The illusion striving to convince me
Of perfection and holiness lost
But merely a dream it was
Giving birth to false thought
Driven by fear to conceal
The divine love thought lost
Yet love, or perfection, or holiness
Cannot flee nor be driven away
Forever a part of us
Eternally owned
Ours to give away

Siren Song

The stretch of thought punctured
The idea of perfection
Led us to see and believe
Greener was the grass outside Heaven

We hear the siren song
The ultimate enticement offers
The treasure beyond the treasure
The more than most
The higher than highest

Perfection becomes insufficient
Eternity is not enough time
The All requires something more
Leaving us with but empty rhyme

Home Sweet Home

It is good to be home
My way lost so often
So many dead ends and u-turns
Falling through emptiness into nothing

Several roads gone down
Many paths well traveled
Experiences to please and perform for
Lies to believe and die for

A confounding place, far too fragile
Shifting sands form no foundation
Sinking here and falling there
Deciding to stand upright
And stay there

For me, no more mis-travels
For me, less time will be spent
On truths falsely given
Only heed paid those Heaven-sent

Constitutional Comfort

The colonists succinctly discarded
Imperialism in the new land
Sought for and fought for a better way
To govern and come together
A way to be and live in peace
Means that would endure and hold fast
A contract required to state
The rules of conduct and rights

So debate they did
These ways to live
These safeguards and premises
The goal to agree to agree
On the charter sublime

With guided pen and thoughts divine
This band of brothers writing as one
Found avenues to freedom
And words to define
High ideals and motives pure
Wanting something more
A masterpiece to inspire and endure
A constitution and rights declared

The brave group long disbanded now
Gone far down history's isles
Only the ideas prevailed
On parchment, under glass
Protected from time

The years have increased, some made finer
The ideals of a golden age
Statesmen have debated and critics assailed
Divine thoughts authored and relevant still

Why have they endured and held fast
And ruled us fairly and best
Perhaps the brothers knew

The source from whence they came
Thoughts intruded upon minds of man
To encourage a higher road
To help brother see brother
When blindness would lead astray
A tome to give pause
When fear would take away
The rights God-given
That sweet American day

John Henry

Born a man, a proud African citizen
Taken from his home by greed and stealth
Leaving a family broken and fatherless
For money, ignorance, and greed

John Henry was strong and black
A large man, tall and imposing he stood
The body of Hercules
The soul of a dove

His family and peace were all he prized
A simple man trying to get along
Fair to his neighbors, a source for all
Living to be good, happy to be alive

Those simple, sweet days gone now
As the slave traders beat and prod
Afraid of the giant, awed by his size
Yet dollars counting, they prized their prize

A gentle man captured by those less so
A tragedy born that day
Hearts broken and sadness reigned
All in a days work and the devil's pay

John Henry cried when left alone
Too proud for the cruel captors to see
His heart heavy as his country faded
His shoreline replaced by one far away

Days of discomfort and strife
Hungry, beaten, robbed of his life
Treated as livestock, meat for sale
Reduced to headcount, his soul grew pale

The long days at sea finally passed
The new home reached at last
Uncertainty and fear his companions now
Sold to rich men, but poorer than he

Placed on the platform for all to see
Bids placed on the man so strong
No smile for the price, no soul of the man
Body purchased and nothing more

The buyers cared not but for profit and use
The soul not of the bargain made
This gentle giant with so much to add
Stood motionless with heart so sad

Sold and purchased as merchant's wares
The property of genteel men with hearts of stone
Branded and named with no care for the man
Only muscles to them, a working machine

Life was hard, the days were long
Picking cotton in the Carolina sun
Side by side with his new family of slaves
Spirit intact and returning to life

They sang as they toiled
And spoke of days gone by
Telling stories of their homeland
And dear ones left behind

The days passed, the years quickly too
John Henry grew older and slower
No longer the machine his owners once prized
Just an old man they had come to know

The plantations thrived under John Henry's toil
Time permitted the landlords to know him well
They could not help but admire the man
Who, through the suffering and labor, stood so tall

His spirit and goodness caused them to pause
And reflect on this giant soul of a man
Even shame sought refuge
As they compared them to him

Come one fine summer day
When John Henry could arise no more
The labor and sadness taking their toll
From the man stolen so very long ago

The master came to his bedside
To say farewell to his aged property
Humbled by one of greater character
He now cried for both souls

John Henry looked on his captor from death's door
Granting him the smile denied before
For a moment before he returned home
Brothers but for an instant
Then John Henry was no more

Technology Magic

Gathering places, now technology oasis
Laughter replaced by keyboard clicks
Many now drawn to the techno-toys
Thoughts placed now in the software mix

For some, it is enough to self-amuse
For others, the need to create commands
Dazzled by the abilities of toys with brains
Seeking faster, bolder, more violent scores

Tiny music boxes on a string
Wired directly to the hearing port
Small video machines to hold the eye
To amaze the brain's report

Seeing more, hearing louder
Moving faster through the maze
Learning only sensory lessons
Losing time from greater days

Settling for so little
We buy the amazements galore
Exciting and amusing
Intrigued by knowledge no more

Little people jumping at play
On a screen of tiny proportions
Missing the full-sized ones ahead
Their thoughts on the I-Phone instead

Computers brought to life by coding
The CPU apes the brain machine
Outperforming the dawdling human
Faster than bodies can be

Yet laptops and handhelds yield but tiny brains
The more mundane functions to perform
Only tasks better lifted from us
Freeing mind from brain's lesser form

So use the mind's newfound freedom
Not for toys or puzzles to solve
But to stretch for a greater reality
To know the mind's truest resolve

Sticks and Stones

Sticks and stones will hurt you
Although hurled from your hand alone
Though the target may be bruised and torn
Your soul to be the poorer of the two

You harm no one besides yourself
To divided sight it seems untrue
Yet injury goes to the soul of the attacker
Harming more than the body bruised

No need to believe in oneness
No call to the skeptic professed
Reality is, believe or not
There for the believer
And those who forgot

We are connected in ways unknown
Forged of the very same mettle
Derived from the very same soul
Brought to boil in the very same kettle

So continue to wound and injure you may
Only to awaken some fine golden day
Eyes then opened wide
To see what the soul has paid

Personal Ambitions

I took daddy's little hammer
And went to building castles
Monuments to ambition
To little me, just a day's play

Later years, it faded to mystery
The goals of those younger days
Building, building, building
Layers of wants and needs

The buildings later became years
And ideas born of those
Gave life to ambition reborn
Set in motion the searching mode

The days came when I knew
I wanted more than I owned
I needed more than provided
Always having less, I bemoaned

The stretching regimen began
The straining from here to there
Becoming less while owning more
Setting sight on the prized career

I walked it long
I walked it tall
Things started happening
All to forestall
The sight of the true path
Open to all

As I walked the walk
And talked the talk
Fortune came, faint glory too
Fully equipped to do what I do

Years of coolness, fun times true
Enjoying the ride galore
The more I like it, the more it goes
The pleasure dimming, poetry to prose

I find myself now
At the end of Ambition Row
The past joys a fading dream
No battles to fight
No brothers as foes

The personal ambition is gone now
Replaced by a variety unknown
To no longer chase or pursue
But to serve the life I deem true

Strange Man

A strange man, I am indeed
Too shy to talk about it
But let me bend your ear awhile
And I'll see to it you understand

To see inside the One Mind
You must know
Is to leave yours behind
As you go

Expanding smaller all the time
Reducing to nothing, emerging to all
No limits to truth, no end in sight
Enter the labyrinth of Heavenly delight

This place I go, I leave port now
Stepping over, the process prescribed
I trust my Captain completely
Standing strangely with the prize

My Captain's Door

Waves are hitting hard
And tossing our ship about
The storm attacks us harshly
The fear begins to mount

The crew is less together now
Allowing fear to push apart
Maritime brothers we were
Seeming less so now

The time to pull together
Most needed in moments of peril
No other recourse given
That will save our ship of fools

And foolish we are and foolish we've been
But now the time approaches
To pull together mates
And awaken as one again

So I knock hard
Against my captain's door
Yet no reply is forthcoming
Silence answers, nothing more

Crew and ship both dissolving
Amid the tough and briny assault
Hope crashing down with the fallen mast
Only dread in common now

I call for my captain
Louder still I yell
Save us from the fate upon us
Let not our journey be to hell!

My voice finally failing
To bring the captain out
My heart and ship are breaking
Finally Heaven's name I shout

My boys pause in their terror
Knowing a divine call had been made
Leaving despair for a moment
Hoping again the storm would fade

A sailor believes in miracles
At times, his only way out
Believing in man or captain
Insufficient counter to the ocean's rage

But mighty sea or thundering skies
Cower down in deference
At the call to a higher power
And make ready to obey it

The maelstrom subsided
The sea at peace again
Men's hearts calmer now
Having witnessed the divine friend
A Captain of larger stature
Who would never fail us again

The Great Play

The play performs us well
This theater of worldly ways
Cast in roles unwanted
Yet insisted upon by all

Several acts has the fearsome play
Started countless eons ago
Involved in the oldest profession
Of acting, in what, we do not know

Life is but a play, the great bard declared
And we but actors upon its stage
Words borrowed again from the master
We share once more this day

Lost in the parts and the play itself
Forgetting who, in truth, we were
Believing the endless script recited
Living only within the scenes replayed

Countless performances well acted
Endless applause offered as pay
Audiences well pleased and delighted
By actors playing them
On the mythical stage

The playhouse becomes reality
The stage an empty home
The players all but shadows
Of brethren lost long ago

If only we could see
Above the stage and play
Beneath the words and actions
What lies beyond the illusion
That keeps us prisoner this day

Look beyond the plays and dreams
To a place where only peace performs
Where love is the only actor
And forgiveness the only fee

Freedom Thought

How ironic the thought of freedom
By minds bound so tightly
By thoughts related in error
To such items of bondage
That would never set us free

How superficial the assumption
Of reality as presented
Being less than it supposes
Seeming more plausible than it proposes

Is it true because it is sighted
It must be, if it is heard
Not likely false, I can touch it
Who knows where it was learned

I'll need to investigate quite thoroughly
No matter how the unlikely the folly
Of such impressions being true

What we know of hallucination
Should prompt our belief in illusion
But only enough to dissolve it
Freedom then, and nearly true

Ultimate I

What am I to be
This man, this body, this life
That so often confuses and fails me
A hollow shell waiting to be filled

A boy, then robust, now older
Growing in ways that matter not
Taller, larger, smarter
Well-schooled in the ways of the world

Better educated, hoping to get rich
Better groomed, hoping to get laid
Buying better wheels to drive me about
Promoting the image of man self-made

I found myself a woman or two
Popped a couple of kids along the way
Bought myself a big ole house
Grew respectable and fit in

Made more money, lost some too
Good investments in the wrong things
Promotions at work made me important
People validating me, made it true

But years kept counting
And glory days started to fade
Less handsome now, weaker too
Self-importance feeling less valuable

Good friends and family as well
Just not connected enough
Money can't buy what I need
I never seem to measure up

I am left here standing
Wealthy but surely impoverished
Healthy but ill at soul
Having everything but nothing

My soul starts to crumble
Mind and emotions collide
Unable to fend for myself
Unsure that I'm happy, or even alive

So many years I hid loneliness
Always solitary, even among friends
The emptiness has followed me
From cradle to promised grave

I stand at a crossroads
Struggling to live or die
Must know the reasons for both
Before I can decide

The day comes when it is all too much
To carry around on sagging shoulders
My soul cries out for another
I know not for whom I yearn

I drop to my knees
And beg for my life
Not for the one given
But for another, unlived

Sadness and grief overcome me
I slip into ebony hell
The bottom of my soul greets me
Promising all will be well

My heart splits, my mind opens
To whatever now welcomes me
Into this light ahead
No fear to delay or abate me

My savior has touched me
And filled my wretched emptiness
Showing me once and for all
The holiness within me
The ultimate I that calls

Mr. Perfect

Perfection, my friend and enemy
Taught by an earnest dad
To brace his son for the world at large
Taught me how to do well
But never well enough

Climbing the ladder of success
Acquiring all wanted and more
Believed it gave what I needed
Kept striving but never fulfilled

Every mistake so painful
Learning to avoid them my goal
Becoming quite good at it
While robbing my soul

Layers of guilt encased me
For not being what I never could be
Perfection unattainable in a world so flawed
My only course forgiveness
Allowing myself to be incomplete

Caring about perfection no longer
My only need to find my soul
To gain what will make me whole

So one day I just dropped it
Laid it all at my Father's feet
Prayed for Him to take it from me
And replace it with Him complete

His light blinded my eyes
His love threatened to burst me
The peace then soothed me
Knowing what was ahead

All those years of regretting
The goal I could never attain
Now all of it behind me
Replaced by perfection gained

Quest for Excellence

Quality sought in all things rendered
Searching for the essence undefined
The measure of all things made
The price of all things fine
Like truth, known when it is found
Not merely a look or finish
An estimate of treasure's merit
A meter to appraise its worth
Looking for any that would excel
Hoping for the one fine thing
That would make us hopeful again
That indefinable something
A single instance of excellence found

The Great Belgium Belch Off

The crowds gathered at sunrise
To witness the annual event
The gathering of all great gas bellies
Belching here and there they went

Warming up for the day's competition
Drinking soda, and beer, and air
Hoping to inflate sufficiently
And retain the belches spared

The crowds grew large and clamored for more
Of the greatest belchers Belgium had ever known
This tiny country with little claim to fame
Playing host to intestinal foam

The contest began at last
Belchers facing belchers
Under glaring spotlights
Amid frantic fans of gas

Louder and grosser the combatants became
Hours of burping took their toll
Bodies lay limp and depleted
Lesser ones belched out and gone

Those left standing all but exhausted
Until at last only two remained
The best of the belchers in Belgium land
They squared off and faced each other
Each determined to out-belch the rest

Rangus McGee, the reigning champ
From the isle of green and Guinness
Facing Big George of England
Self-taught at London's finest pubs

Rangus went first as custom bound
Drank his pint and held his breath
Leaving the crowd cheering and waiting
For the inevitable blast at last

The tension mounted as Rangus held on
Face turning red as the hair on his head
The great belch on its way now
Unfettered, it roared from his mouth

Silence followed the belch supreme
The fans stunned and amazed
At what Rangus had rendered that day
A belch for the ages, leaving all dazed

Rangus now done and quite pleased
With the performance of a lifetime
Confident he had conquered
Yet another opponent less ventilated

Big George stood and hushed the crowd
His size and belly, both quite grand
He took no beverage, no aid of any kind
Simply reared back and belched his all
That left none standing, nor windows intact

Big George stood surveying the mess
That his extraordinary eructation created
He had bested the best
Poor Rangus deflated
Defeated at last

Rebel Yell

Blood running from me
Into the dirt, my bed
An unusual place to die
An unfit burial ground

It seems like so long ago
When a mere boy I was
Running through those golden fields
Riding ole Bess to school

Then one day the soldiers came
Stern faces accepting no objection
Insisting we join them or else
To defend our sovereign nation

So daddy, Bruce, and I departed
From our beloved Carolina home
Donned the woolen grey suits
That marked us rebels all

Mama's crying, Sissy too
Left man-less and defenseless
Tears in all eyes, ours too
So sad, and proud, and scared

The first day wasn't so bad
A few shots and cannons away
Still no blood flowing
No wounds to slay

By mid morning of the next
My brother lay in my arms
Nearly breathless and speechless
His life seeping away

The Lord took him that day
Bruce's blood on my sleeves
The darkness had dawned
My life would never be the same

Before the day ended
I had lost my daddy too
A hole in his head, instantly dead
In one short day, three became one

From that day onward
I never really cared
If bullet or bayonet forced me
To join my men folk at Heaven's gate
At least that's where I hope we go
When I leave this world so foul
I'll know the answer shortly
Farewell, my fallen friends

A Thought Never Dies

Pause for a moment
Reflect on what it is
That makes us who we are
Separate from the rest

But if a different form
Makes us solitary souls
We need to inquire within
To see if truth unfolds

In moments rare but true
The body disappears
Leaving only what is real
Devoid of any fear

One Mind blended of many thoughts
We are those thoughts, my friend
Discard the useless forms
And let our souls begin again

My Neighbor's House

The man next door loves me
Though he knows it not
His grey haired mistress does too
But she likely forgot
Few words are spoken
Mainly nods and smiles
Acknowledging each other
Agreeing to be false pals
But nothing more it seems
And barely friends the theme
Until we look inside each other
And witness the related we

"A fine back yard you have there"
"Yours too" they say at once
"Love your house" say I
"And yours as well" replied

Candle Light Thirty Years Later

A day on snow-capped mountain
Beautifully spent and well-viewed
Coming to a close quite soon
Cooling sun saying *adieu*

Darkness ensues
Until now, hidden from view
Shadows growing larger
Few sun places show through

In a single moment
A light did appear
Neither coming nor going
It was simply resident here

A warm glow returning
The darkness retreats from light
The shimmering glow continues
To show the face of Christ

Painless Birth

Everything sends the wrong signal
When nothing comes from light
Chaos surrounds the event
Darkness rules the night

When babies come to mommies
It seems a blessed event
Bearing witness to an arrival
Appearing in the soul's intent

Wrapped in body, the soul encased
Hoping to eliminate the shame as waste

Conceived in pleasure
Birthed in pain
The double-edged sword
Too sharp to contain

Someday the moment will come
When birth to Heaven is prized
One of peace and completion
Natured of joy, love, and life

No pain in this resurrection
No crying amid the blood
Only pure happiness offered
And true home, forever One

I Love Baseball

I love the game of baseball
The truest sport of man and men
So many parts all working together
Each precisely, to gain the game

The power of the batter
Opposing the pitcher's speed
Both outguessing the other
With foolery un-banned indeed

The hurler intimidates
With pitches so close
The hitter can feel them
Whiz by his nose

First a high fastball
And then one down low
Next a fluttering knuckler
How can one know

Yet batter casts the final vote
Curveball or slider
At home in catcher's mitt
Or travel-bound, on a rope

The connection missed
Confirmed by the backstop's grunt
Ninety-eight mile an hour fastballs
Greets leather with one helluva pop

But the pitcher shakes it off
Readies himself again
Bracing for his opponent's best stuff
Hoping his is good enough

This time the pitch is slower
But rotation will tell the tale
Of a ball that goes left or right
And if the batter will fail

Alas, contact is made
Again, that cherished sound
Of golden wood meeting and greeting
Orb-shaped leather found

Off on its journey, the ball begins
The batter now runner, starting his

The ball soaring towards the outfield
Runner streaking for first
That bean just kept going
No destination rehearsed

More than a gentle breeze that day
Resisted the ball's long flight
Took it upon itself to decide
There would be no home run this night

The centerfielder, happy for the chance
To pursue and retrieve the sphere
That seemed destined to elude his glove
And make the fence barely cleared

That wonderful round orb
Bound in leather and thread
Flying towards intersection
With a brown leather hand

The ball arrived in glorious fashion
A monster liner still alive
Nearly four hundred feet it traveled
Home run bound, streaking across the sky

The ball fell short of the fence
As it barely tipped the edge
Of a racing fielder's glove
Dribbling away, an unanticipated fate

Runner now headed for third
Visions of a triple danced in his head
But no deal was made
No agreement reached
On the outcome of this duel
And the fate of these men

The ball finally found
And ready to throw
The orb badly battered
Back into the fray it goes

Quickly retrieved and soon delivered
Slicing through the ballpark air
A mighty toss engendered
A play at third insured

The runner began his slide
Hard and fast into the baseman
The ball arriving in the nick of time
Destined to be a close one

Bodies clash, soggy bag ajar
Runner, baseman, ball, and dirt
Coming together, converged at once
The umpire too, to make the call
Arms spread wide to avoid confusion
"Safe!" he yelled for all to hear
We have ourselves a triple, people
Now pause and wait for cheers

One Again

I cried for Heaven lost
And I cried for Heaven found
For all the wasted years
And for coming home at last

I emptied all that bound me
And all that kept me apart
I rejoiced for where I now was
And wept for those still lost

I am much lighter now
The weight of worldly ego gone
Only the love of my Father remains
And the family left behind

Join me dear brother
Come to where I am
Hold my hand, touch my heart
Let us be one again

Velvet Pearls

Soft velvet sack, tiny and fine
Caressing sweet pearls
Bag opened wide
As much as I can accept
Comes softly out to opening hand
To warm and englow all it touches
Pearls of wisdom, love-colored rubies
Emeralds so green, grasses envy
Diamonds as brilliant
As Christ thoughts in Mind
Endless blessings forever
Love beyond time

Captain's Orders

I will follow you, my Captain
From here to wherever you say
My allegiance quite voluntary
My direction here to stay
To ocean's upheavals
Or volcanic eruptions
I'm yours to command, O' Captain
Heaven bound my final orders
I can see blindly now
That your timing and heart are true
Your total consideration
My comfort assured and due
From the beginning of time
To the ends of the earth
My footsteps will follow
All signs and orders given
Directing me to my birth

Weep No More

Dry your eyes, you girly man
Suck it up, rub some dirt in it
Be a man, little man

This ego that taunts us so
And shows so little respect
Is nothing to be concerned about
It has so little breadth
A shallow form, illusion at best
Not wanting to admit
Its very obvious deficiencies
Still wanting to make us quit

You're no good little man
You've failed and you always will

A voice so lacking in truth
Reverberates away and dies
Leaving brothers without false audio
Or impressions to follow blindly
Leaving room for better guidance
The angelic song becoming clear
Til long last has finally encountered
The inevitable delay in rushing
Headlong in a direction
Given by voice and heart so frail
Listen instead my brother
To the angel's whispers
And Spirit's breath
To Christ's thought
Becoming your own

The Truest Three

The three I admire the most
The Father, Son, and Holy Ghost

I admit freely the larceny
My brother's words stolen so blatantly
By license granted from the Source of the words
I write them now for all to see
Be at peace brother author and poet
I will treat them with true grace
It kind of sums it up for me
I will give them favored place

This holiest of Trios as One
They are in turn and in whole
My Father and Creator
My blessed Guide and Captain
My beloved Brother and myself
We all belong to the Assemblage described
Blessed Parts, beloved Whole
All in one, One in All

The Verdict

I may need to admit
That I once hated
And may still
An unknown enemy assailant
A friend disguised as foe
But in truth no one ever hurt me
For no one can assail in truth
And no one attacks another
Without himself first accused
All of us found guilty
By a tribunal of all our friends
All bound over for sentencing
For the original sin
But a dream it all was
Believe it we all should
For it still occurs among us
Guilty or not, the illusion stood
Invalidates no verdict in Heaven
One way or another, we all still get in

Come a Day

Come a day
Might as it may
Cause me a disturbance
Cause me to pray
For what I know not
But I must I am certain
Come to this place
The locale undetermined
To stand ready to step over
To pray and wait
Something draws me out
Ever since time was late
From the day grace was lost
And the moment we fell
Into the deepest dream possible
Into our darkened cell
But all dreams need awakening
And this no exception to the rule
Father and Brother gently shaking me
To arise and follow their rule

I'm So Special

I'm so very special, it's clear
All it takes is a look to know
How can you deny such an obvious sight
Just take a look around
And you'll see by note of comparison
How much better I look and am
I am quite handsome
Fairly well off as well
Dressed in only the most popular garb
My fragrance unavoidable
I make lots of money too
I drive those fabulous wheels
I'm quite the package for sure
All I am exudes success
I can hardly stand it myself
If I were any more special
The world would tear me apart
Package me in little pieces
So everyone could own a part

Quite a shell certainly made
But empty of all that would make it
Not special at all, yet holy
Not handsome at all, but divine
Not rich, just owner of all
Not admired so much
As loved eternally and completely

This vehicle I have no use for
I can be wherever I would be
The looks are just a package
That with vision no one can see

I must commend you, my friend
On the cosmetic appeal you have
I only ask that you give it away
And come with me this day
We will lay aside all seductions

All finery and forms well made
Disregard all the lovely adornments
Trade them in for everything true
Replaced by a loving God's gifts
No longer special, just the real you

Dust to Dust

It comes and it goes
One day up, the next day down
Life on earth never the same
Nothing to count on, nothing remains

We search for truth
In an ever-changing world
Looking for certainty
Where none exists

There remains the possibility
That we look and search in vain
Our scope defined by limits
What we seek cannot be feigned

All the things we've made
And ego constructions too
Designed to hide and conceal
Anything born of truth

A futile search indeed
An effort without reward
Time to shift our focus
To eternal things internal

Nothing here endures
And likely never will
We may decide at some point future
To let it return to what it is

Dust to dust, the bible says
An insight into illusion's core
We endlessly shape the fraudulent powder
Into something to need, want, or adore

There is a question worth posing
A valid reason to inquire within
Do we settle for more of nothing
And accept that offered as sin

Magnificent Bodies

I watched in awe the Olympics
Bodies twisting, diving, and such
A magnificent display of ability
Performing in so many ways
Then the thought occurred to me
Of how proudly we judge the event
And of all the admiration applied
To the perfect bodies we rent
But why I ask myself
Do we value this flesh so much
Why is it so important to us
And why do we love its touch
Even us mere amateurs
We do our best to compete
To shed some weight when possible
To muscle up and be so sleek
The days at the health club
The nights spent running and biking
The treadmills and stair steppers
The weights, the climbing, and hiking
To pay homage to the body deluxe
We spend our time and fortune
Discarding other valuables
In quest of our own approval
Why are we so obsessed it seems
With such a meaningless thing
Trying to polish an illusion
Instead of pursuing our King
Many years have passed in the chase
Many more lest I stop it now
I think I will seek a different route
Wherever my soul allows

Fat and Ugly

I am fat and I am ugly
And I don't really care
I dress real funny
And will not compare
To all those graceful lovelies
That I follow with admiring eyes
That I wish I were instead of me
All those sexy abs
All those perfect pecs
Make me want to rush right out
And buy a part or two
Maybe a health club membership
Maybe a tuck or a peal
Anything to make me better
If only I were taller and slimmer
But I would likely need a transplant
Of the hair lost long ago
And a nose far less conspicuous
Less wrinkles to make me smooth
I wonder how much it will cost me
How much I will need to give up
To obtain my newly desired package
A man made over that much
Well I guess I could take another
Job or two to pay
For all those lovely enhancements
Working more would leave me less
Time to sit around and bemoan
How fat and ugly I am
And how little I really care

54

Spilled Milk

I spilled a glass of milk
A usually insignificant event
But for one so long in anger
A triumph of late intent

I guess you would need to know me
To be aware of my soul's bent
For long have I battled anger
The curse of my spirit rent

This same small incident
A year or life ago
Would have taken me to rage's door
Scarring my soul, my spirit left poor

The cursing and swearing
That damned my children's ears
Now left behind forever
With rage, and guilt, and fear

Baby Lights

Created by Christ
Written by me
So honored and blessed
Its scribe to be
These poems and writings
Are like children to me
Wonderful light creatures
Dressed in words of glee
A painless and joyful birth has each
These thoughts brought to terms
The pen a conduit of ink imbued
Where fluid of truth intrudes
Now upon paper for all to see
Words addressed from other worlds
Divine thoughts are honored to carry
Truth to minds unfurled

Disbelieve

We choose our beliefs
Believe it or not
All paths directed
By one mind or two
Our real choice belongs
Not to this or that
But only to the mind
We choose to use in fact
All born of one great Mind
When the gift was first given
But chase we did another
At Eden's gate departed
A much smaller mind we elected
Devoid of all that was true
A simple calculator
Yet brilliant in deception
Self-preservation its goal
The tiny mind just an illusion
But follow it for eons we did
Led us down the primrose path
Away from Heaven's gate
Towards a deadly fate
Suffering and pain it bequeathed
Emptiness and solitude as well
Hollow gifts indeed
For such souls as God once gave
Do not despair my brother
Resolve to choose again
Ask for that divinely offered
Truth devoid of sin

One Judge Only

No longer good people or bad
Nevermore shall I attempt to judge
Any person by their features
Nor by stature will I condemn
So many differences, so much the same
Difficult to make sense of it
Impossible to judge as sane
No way to know what fits
No way to judge aright
So why do we often try
And why do we always fail
Perhaps we know so little
About brother or sister in truth
So difficult for us to tell
So far from real it hurts
This world will make us crazy
If we try to figure it out
No truthful way to judge another
I say let's leave it to God
Let Him figure it out

Insufficient Pairs

Odd it seems
In a world of opposites
So many pairs
But nothing whole

Man and woman
Brother and sister
Black and white
Good and bad

Why have we not noticed
That nothing is quite complete
Futile efforts at merging
A seemingly impossible feat

Should it not be different
This insufficiency we own
Should we not be together
Should we not be whole

Pairs of opposites abound
They seem somehow deliberate
Failing often to satisfy
Clues of oneness unfound

We settle for so little
In this fractured place we call home
Learning to abide in isolation
Content with half not whole

I propose we raise our standards
And look for something new
The search however ancient
Leads us to Eden true

Our Father is whole and complete
He includes us all as well
In truth, we are but equals
In truth, we are paired as One

Humpty Dumpty

The Holy Spirit is here
To put Humpty Dumpty
Back together again
Not a bad egg altogether
Just broken and cracked
In need of just repair
Fallen from walls so high
Down to earth in a sudden way
Could have bounced he might
If made of a more resilient shade
The Beloved reaches down
To retrieve the broken shell
And restore right away
The wholeness of the egg

A Silent Way

I say what I need to say
In a poetic way
Words becoming notes
Played in a melodic way
Phrases become whispers
In a silent way

Gay Man

It matters so little
That it doesn't count at all
Whether you lie with woman or man
The gender an illusion anyway
The sex but folly and play

Don't define yourself my brother
In terms that serve you not
Sexuality is but one aspect
Of the myth well-spun

There is so much more to you
Than a slender term implies
So much more to give than time

Let us set aside all differences
And admit how little they say
Move ahead and beyond
To the sameness and oneness
Gifted to all, gender away

Man on a Wire

High above the landscape
Rooftops appear below
A man looks down upon us
Makes ready to walk on air
He seems so calm, so at ease
As he stares at the depths below
What brought him here
To this time and place
Preparing to balance on wire
To walk where no one has tried
To be above the average pedestrian
To do what could only be imagined
To do what few would dare
What drives such a man
To such feats up high
Why must he do this thing
Perhaps his way to fly
Looking deep inside before the feat
To challenge both courage and means
To decide for one last time
If it is worth his death to him
For demise is what he wagers
This gamble with prize unknown
Yet something drives him to it
He obeys his chosen call
Perhaps he will know someday
What moves him to do such things
To risk his life this way
The man on a wire makes ready
The first step the hardest to take
Beyond that there is no decision
Beyond that he meets his fate
He moves to position untethered
Just him, the wire, and his pole
One step at a time is taken
Each could be his last
Like life lived well in time
He lives only in the moment

Each step defines his life
Or ends in body broken
Where he finishes at end of stride
Not his to know or even decide

New Employer

My new employer
Immediately bequeathed me
People to love and care for
A family to become part of
A place to fit in and find out
What awaits us all
And what due is to come of it
Connections formed on day first joined
Brothers retracing steps
On paths ancient borne
Giving way to the divine pull
The urge to merge, so to speak
The feel and the thought of it
Holds enormous appeal
Our natural state as brothers
Rejoining the One, our Source
This is what Heaven is
This is what is

Ode to a Prostitute

Sad sister, lift up your eyes
Let nothing assail you
For sin has never attached you
You are more than you know
Not less by what you sell
The body matters not
Only a vehicle to move us
From where we are
To where we want to be
But your soul, sweet sister
Matters profoundly to me
So sell it not for any token
It belongs to only you
No one but God may lay claim
Not for human fools

Wall of Illusion

It's as if we are
Running furiously to maintain
The crank speed of the generator
That projects the wall of illusion
Fear must drive us, I believe
To work so hard for so little
When all we truly need
We already have within us
Take a break, my brother
Ease off that mesmeric handle
Inhale deeply, let go lightly
Be at peace within
And without will follow shortly
The endless instant
The being of love
Will bring us sweet salvations
Cause the wall to crumble down

Barren Space

The room's bareness greeted me
With little to offer of grace
It seemed to want to ignore me
Too much decoration, I guess

It spoke in the most direct of terms
Barren words carry no meaning
It pointed to the bed at length
As if to show me
Even in death, I could not be
Welcomed to this place
Of bare uncertainty

Stripped bare of its linens and quilts
Now cousin to the room so bare
The bed's emptiness made me sad
As if to emphasize
No comfort to be had
No home place offered
No place to lay my head

We will look past its emptiness
With vision seeing only the divine
We brush away the dreary scene
Barren no more, the sun to shine

Cheap Thrills

What fires our imagination
What stokes the fire within
What do we live for
What makes us new again
The sights I see
The sounds heard too
All to excite and bedazzle
None of it rings true
Put them all together
And package in life so taut
The reason we stay here
Sadly alone and lost
But I can assure you
Twas not excitement or pain
Cheap thrills omitted
Not part of the plan
We value so little
And so little makes us smile
Gleaming faces a mask
For deep sadness inside
Continue on we do
Settling for what we know
Yet knowing so little
Of what our soul does show
Pleasure will give way
To the pain it hides
Replace by joy and forgiveness
Confusion mediated inside
Sadness gone
Only the joy is true
So very much more
Our souls entitled to
While bodies and egos
Insist on bondage
To a world untrue
Know this, brother and sister
We have everything we need
To make us divinely happy
Nothing cheap we need heed

Quest for Home

The poet-philosopher moves on
His journey far from made
Clothing soon to be tattered
His path along seldom ways
Likely no one to clothe him
Or feed him for a sonnet's pay
He seeks truth as we all do
His, the more pointed way
Trying to see from God's point of view
Expressing it in words imbued
With grace from above
And fire from within
He prays for truth
He seeks a better way
His journey quite simple
All maps contained within
The knowledge he explores for
Bound not by experience or tome
It envelopes and consumes him
His, the quest for Home

Rumi and the Rest

Brother found at last
Hoping to join the rest
Truth keeps showing me
All that is best

A poet newly born am I
Fairly unfamiliar to those
Who pen words finely divined
And visit where few will go

Now that I have found
My chosen way and truth
I seek to shake hands in comfort
With poets and wordsmiths too

One morning they came true
Poetic figures all
Knocking at my doorway
Bid enter, one and all

I wrote much before
The urge to read it swelled
Into a merging that showed me
That knowledge was a golden pail

I listened to Bob Dylan
A poet of caustic terms
But just below the edges
Lies truth in fearless words

I replayed the songs of the minstrel
Van Morrison, his earthy name
An artist of many talents
Not the least a poet's fame

And then the name of Rumi
Brought my eyes to brother true
His heart and mind on Heaven
Words born of spirit come through

His love is my love
And yours as well to share
Sweet Christ speaking through
Glorious Persian ancient fair

Poets Don't Get Rich

Not a lucrative trade by any means
No path to worldly success
But neither do they matter
For grace is all we gather

Now let me not mistake you
For someone naive to lies
For I have both trade and fortune
And worldly ways refined

My path to here not likely
A shy but seeking boy
Of all that the world offered
And my daddy thought true

I fared quite well
In the world and what it offered
Many years made good use of it
Sat on pillows and combed my hair

But all of it was nonsense
A house of mirrors was all I saw
Showed me nothing to believe in
Nothing worthwhile at all

Cynical and blind I became
Later years tempered me tame
All things falsely given
Brought only despair and pain

So now I make my money
From the day's labor and thought
Only a requirement now
No longer needed or sought

The act of caring for nothing
Delivered the gift of All
Laid down what the world offered
Reclaimed my poet's call

Thoughts Worth Thinking

What do you choose to think
Alone with aspirant unanswered
For a choice it surely is
Of this you must learn to know

Thoughts enter only at our beckoning
Responding to invitation alone
In truth there are two minds
One small, one large, we own

As befitting a world of pairs
The smaller brought us here
And feeds the thoughts unending
Made it did, a world of fear
With rage and pain defending

The larger mind defies description
Its beauty unimaginable
The purity of its being
Commendation enough for any

Time to decide, dear brother
Delay not in fearful silence
Choose the Mind that made you
And thoughts divinely lent

Papa's Little Princess

Sweet fresh miss
Gliding across green grasses
Barely touching the world
Yet lighting as she passes

Her face a place
For joy to shine
Her heart and soul
A treasure so fine

Honor-bound and Heaven blessed
Her royal guard I am appointed
My life to guide and teach her
My soul to reach and feed her

My precious child and holy charge
Gently born and tendered
Forever we share each other
Father-Daughter, Sister-Brother

No Strain, No Tears

Infinitely varietous
Yet always the same
Consistent and eternal
Boundless and inclusive
Chaste love and freedom
Bird's flight on loftiest air
Purest water streaming
Most brilliant of roses
Fragrance lavender fed
Completely free and safe
Nothing to lose or die for
All to embrace and prayed for
Knowing all, being as is
Truth found and endeared
No strain, no tears

Retreat from Fear

Walk away from fear, my brother
It offers nothing you would own
Leading only to darkness
The opposite direction of home

Face it we must
And know its hollow power
Yes, frighten us it does
The phantom that bids us cower

A brick in the wall of illusion
As dense and hard as we make it
Yet truth will allow us entry
To walk quickly and safely through it

Our retreat to darkness
Leads us around the wall
Only to meet another
Our destiny to forestall

Retreat we do in many ways
So disoriented we flail about
Dodges and escapes aplenty
Hoping the fear is without

But know the wall is within us
Maintained by ego's will
An imagined wall of lies
Which only light will dispel

Run not back to the womb either
Nor to worldly pursuits
Sex or money cannot hide you
From that which haunts and eludes

Turn instead to One who loves you
Who with but whisper of breath
Assumes the alter offered
Brings love to vanish the rest

Beloved Friend

There is a friend we all know
The truest of all we are
Who never fails to help us
A friend who carries us far

He has always been beside us
For you see, there is no other way
He is as much a part of us
As ourselves in every way

He does not appear before us
No clothes or body He wears
He simply resides within us
Our soul with whom he pairs

Awaken some day we will
And see our brother fair
Never again to doubt the friend
Who with God we share

Counterfeit World

Buckets of beliefs
Fixed containers of thought constrained
Formed from false world experience
Born of rules that restrain

Much of what we believe
Is very likely untrue
Layer upon layer of concepts
Ideas bound by dimensional boxes

Trained from earliest entry
Into a counterfeit world
Beliefs passed by word of mouth
And convention blindly accepted

Heard enough and told enough
We accept assumptions unfounded
By only material consensus
We all agree to agree

Ever the argument ensued
By the two faces of illusion's creed
Conflict continuously engendered
Hard to imagine a world less cruel
Than one which enforces
Such matters as these ugly rules
It would be another matter
If they cared for and served us well
Provided grounds for growth and comfort
Instead they carry famine of spirit
And stifling disease of mind
Nothing to feed the soul
Nothing to expand the restrictions imposed
The goal to contain the limitless
To affirm the counterfeit world
To maintain and strengthen
The dream's hold and fixation

The mind remains captive
To false beliefs and ideas
Of what really exists
And of where we belong

Challenge them all my friends
Make them prove their worth
See if they hold up to scrutiny
Insist that they endure
For if they fail to satisfy
And give lives unfulfilled
Let us shake them off at once
And let truth be our guide

Our Creator has so much more to offer
A world consistent and true
Rules that abide our spirit
Faith that never fails us
A mind that will ever amaze us
In a home forever safe and real
A place that knows no opposites
For all is one and agrees
To live in peace and harmony
Unbound and floating free

Blessings Given

To share the blessings given
Is my joy and duty found
For love cannot restrain
Or in any way be bound

The gifts divinely bestowed
Must be given away as such
The only intent of gifts of love
To inspire the Art of One

Far too precious to hoard
Much too plentiful to contain
The blessings freely given
To make us beautifully sane

Bonding brother to brother
Infusing all with love's consent
Blessing all in time and forever
This is what our Father sent

Sixty Arrived

Today is my birthday
Sixty years in body and place
Raced through so many
Places and people and things

So many experiences, both good and bad
Frivolous opportunities, more to be had
Bumps and bruises, mistakes and pain
Nothing to lose, nothing to gain

Avenues traveled in search of truth
Starts and stops, u-turns too
Friendships and marriages, children as well
Odd patterns delivered, directing towards hell

Beliefs accepted and born on my own
Many proven quite false
Excitement readily available
Pleasures bought at a cost

Detained quite often
Never my goal or intent
Stumbling and falling
Along my life's way
Seeking and finding
At last, a true way

My Father has found me
Lost long on wind-tossed sea
Filled my life completely
By letting me clearly see
All that was missing
All that is free
All love's blessings
All that is me

Traditional Obscurity

I ask myself upon writing
Just what this means to me
This errant thought and visitor
Of traditional obscurity

Somehow my mind knows
And soon will reveal
The mystery that approaches
And causes me such appeal

Enough at least
To arise and write
These mystical lines
Of obscurity's might

I know not what I scribe
Just written as it arrives
Quite unorthodox it seems
Hidden within obscurity's seams

Will we reveal this, my story
That robs me of my sleep
Will convention be damned
To relative obscurity

The riddle continues
Giving no room to pause
In our thinking about it
This puzzle to solve

Well dear friends
Now I must admit
I have little to offer as answer
Only ideas strongly bent

Let not your mind race around it
Nor concern your relative peace
Simply eliminate the nonsense
Of traditional obscurity

Prayer For My Brother

Bless my brother, dear Father
For she is me, I am her
Inseparable, indivisible
Not many or few, just one
It matters not how she looks
Or what she says or does
The crucial part between us
Is what it means to Thee
To You, I surmise no difference
Between her form or mine
Bodies' illusion avoids true sight
To You, we are united
The one Son, holy made
Bless my brother, my Father
Bless us both we pray

Ego's Eye

God's life is simple
The way to it easy as pie
For the world never happened
Except in ego's eye

All that ever was
And all that ever is
Has never left us homeless
Except in egos' eye

Heaven awaits our return
We need only accept it
Let go all that would hide it
Behind egos' eye

Our choice is simple really
No toil or price to pay
Let the Christ Mind direct us
Replace ego's eye this day

I Am Worthy

I am worthy of my Father's Love
I am worthy of His gifts
I deserve all He has given
Redeemed by all I am
Heaven as home belongs to me
This world I deny as true
I am deserving of so much more
Than belittles the Son of God
I throw off the bonds
Of body and ego lies
I dedicate myself to truth alone
A quest quite worthy indeed
We are all His children, my brothers
A child of one in truth
We are all so worthy of each other
Deserving all that is true

California Gift

A child deprived of a father's love
The mother's love diminished too
By lack of love to give
Though loved she was, in truth

This love-orphan we invited in
Though less accepting at the time
Our will not yet offered
To a greater wisdom than mine

But transcend it we did
As we said those words so dear
Thy will be done, my Father
That freed our hearts from fear

The bouncy baby with curls so fair
Entered our lives that day
Regret left through the very same door
The blessing unannounced remained

Since that glorious California day
Our lives and we, never the same
So much more than asked for
Sweet Sasha was her name

Time and Space and Things

Since ancient times began
We have known time, and space, and things
What and how have they served us
Or have we served them instead

Know we not a better way
A better truth in its place
Pull away from things we must
Obviate time, denying space

Look for something more real
Something that endures and unites
Learn to admit we know nothing
Leaving time and space behind

The Swallows

In tight-knit circles
In streams of graceful wings
Flashes of color in motion
Forms of brilliant things

They flew closer and closer
Greeting us in twinkling cadence
Embracing us, and we them
In love ever since

Beloved child beside me
Sharing it with aging papa
Both graced by the holy moment
Watched by the ancient agama

Open your mind to the wonder
Widen your heart to contain
Accept the natural gift offered
Rendered by the swallows' refrain

American Brothers

John and Thomas were brothers true
So different in every way
The oddest couple formed
Born of the American fray

One was short and squat
The other tall and slender
One outspoken and direct
The other quiet and enigmatic

Possessing beliefs that could surely separate
Superseded by a love that allowed it not
Different paths seemed destined
But again, the bond prevailed

Though the philosophy differed
And the worldly ways diverged
Neither could trump the love
That bound them together as one

They suffered together
In concert they were tried
But forever brothers they were
Until the same day they both died

Long Lost

Fair Indian friends
Gentle, kind, and polite
Bringing back elegance to America
Returning the long lost light

We seem to have lost the touch
That comes so naturally to you
Your soft intelligence and joy
Reminds me of love held true

You move about gracefully
Filled with color and flow
Leaving arrogance behind
With quiet confidence you go

Helping us to remember
And finally embrace
The elegance and quiet
Of a long lost grace

Chasing Balloons

We go storming through life
No idea of what to do
Like a giant steamroller
Flattening all likely potential
We dash about
Like we know what we are doing
Cover countless miles
Like we know where we go
We flail about, thrashing and turning
From one belief balloon to another
They float just beyond our grasp
We settle for the vision departing

Golden Boy

Sweet golden boy
Heroic you seem
The light unrestrained
The love refusing to be contained
My sweet beloved son
Born one fine October day
You're gone now amid the angels
I am left behind, to follow some day
A short time on earth bound us
As our paths converged and held us
Together for part of the way
Some good-turning we carry this day

Whispering Wind

What I think, then dare say
Is meant for some, or all, or none
It matters so very little
The words will find their place

Strike a nerve here, a note over there
The key to the waiting time-lock
Hoping for a perfect convergence
Of past and future, and now

The words are carried on soft voices
Falling on waiting ears
Whispers in the wailing wind
And finding their home
They end

Broken Compass

I know not where to go
Nor whether to drive or fly
So often led astray
To places strange and forbidden
Stumbling often, hoping to feel my way
Along highways and byways
Exploring new adventures and beliefs
Searching for pointers and true direction
The rudder is bent, the compass broken too
I ask for my captain, he does not appear
I have much need for direction
My soul without it, sinks into fear
Show me dear Father
The way I must go
No longer a rambler
True north is my goal

True Magician

Purveyor of trickery and deceit made fun
A manipulator of props, perceptions too
A little more here, less over there
Convinced we saw three, yet in truth only two

Born to amuse and bewilder
The man with the magnificent magic
Uncovering things unseen
Waving wands to set things free

Many years, many shows
His craft performed quite well
Yet tricks repeated endlessly
Drain the soul of joyful hope

Growing older now
Less thought for the magic
Time and repetition now a tarnish
Nothing to replace the work
No wife or children to grace him

As his last seed of importance withered
Only to languish and fade
He went to his knees to ask for
Grace to be delivered
Christ to redeem him
The Father to embrace his soul

The prayer continued unceasing
His heart now faithfully exposed
Placed it upon the alter
For the Holy Spirit to compose

Light turned to darkness
Hope shied away
The magician about to lose faith
When Christ touched his face

The touch forever holy
Love shared freely without delay
Only room for one way now
One path left to follow

Many memories lost that day
Yet many more regained
Cleansed of the worldly way
Ready now for the divine filling

The Prince there to console him
Nearby for comfort required
Imparting wisdom unbounded
To the rejuvenated magician
Now himself, a Prince reborn

The Audience Poetic

Audiences both large and small
Addressed them as best provided
Hoping to please them all
Worked hard to deliver
A message worthy of reflection
Sometimes knowing, sometimes not
What came on stage before me
Should come back slowly
For delivery to those of lot
We never know to whom we speak
Words appointed to separate ears
Perception, that nasty little filter
Changing truth and imposing fears
But for me now, sitting here
I know my audience is found
The poet's heart yearns to touch
The Soul Poetic bound

Paradoxical Pairs

So often confused
So very befuddled
Just when I think I have it
The other refutes it
I think I know
Then wisdom says, *no*!
I feel I am fair
And love says, *not enough!*
I believe I am clear
Then the light shows me mistaken
But I know I am holy
And God smiles in agreement

Everyone Wants to Know

However disinterested we may seem
Concerning questions of life unanswered
Our indifference is but fleeting
Our attention destined to return
To the very simple question
Of why and of what we yearn

Avoiding the crucial question
Leaving philosopher or poet to inquire
Hoping life will provide the clues
Leaving nothing else required

Several ways appointed to reject it
Taking forms of pleasure and pain
Substituting what or who
Perhaps a where or when will do

Yet when the queries are answered
Time and time again
None offer viable solution
To the emptiness within

Turn at last to the unasked question
Receive the truth that beckons
Open the mind so long held fast
To holy notions of what may last

Turn now to possibilities unknown
And ask
Not who, or when, or where, or if
Request simply what is left to know
Of life and the soul's great mystery

Why are we here and why must we know
Why am I lonely and why do I grow old
Why do we attack and harm each other so
Why has God left me empty and alone

The answer will surprise I'm sure
For the questions are unfounded and false
If only we may discard them
In favor of what graces our cause

The illusion of the world blinds us
Veiled minds and souls who would know
That God is in and around us
Waiting only for questions to cease
To give ourselves over to Him
And then to know His Peace

The Prince

Born of greatness, grandeur sure
Son of the only God
Prince of the kingdom
Eternal ingredient of the One

Dream of madness, nightmare born
Pulled from heaven, lost in darkness
The way seemed lost
The vision now gone
Pity descended upon the prince

Years of sadness, years of loss
Regret aplenty succeeded the fall
Half alive until grace restored him
Now once again, one with All

Twenty Years Together

Twenty years together, all of them quite fair
I don't know what I would've done without them
Who could have been a more unlikely pair
Yet we somehow managed to do it
Two lives lived quite well
Both of us with much to be proud of
Each to the other we tell
We loved each other truly
And I believe we always will
Touching ever so lightly
The soul with each as well
My beloved Father put you here
To aid and guide me home
Someone to love and be loved by
I hope I have done the same
You are my sweet Tam, my love
My angel graced from above
So if God may tender us gently
With twenty more or so
I would be eternally grateful
To stay with you as we go
From this place that brought us together
To the Home we both love so

No More Honorable Men

Something lost from more honorable times
The character of men forgotten
The lack most evidently exemplified
In those we elect to lead

Character now only something
To be assailed and bent
No room remains for reason
No need felt to repent

Our so-called leaders show us
Much of what taints our souls
And makes us less as people
Makes us less than whole

Attack, the primary strategy
The issues all but lost
The one less smeared remains standing
A cheerless example to us all

The excuse is always given
That to rule we must surely pay
In terms of character lost
The soul not so easily reclaimed

We may still be the finest country
The bar has fallen that low
To allow us our arrogance
Precious else left to show

So wave the red, white, and blue, my fellows
Sing the American cheer
But don't fail to look more closely
At the legacy we all leave here

Many of earth's brothers detest us
Why, we should ask ourselves
Is it our shining example

Or what we have betrayed
We best stop waving
Money and power in the faces
Of those we claim to save

Let's raise the bar again, America
And return to truths self-evident
Be our brother's keeper
Let the eagle soar again

My Life Complete

If I may bring my brother
Just one step closer
To the Home where we are one
I would give my life to do so
And consider it complete

Wouldn't It Be Nice?

If,

No one owned anything
We were one, not more
We felt like babies and played like toddlers
We viewed the mountains and ocean at once
The sun stayed out when it rained
No one was broken
Everyone played baseball
We all lay in the warm sun with cool breezes
We could see forever
Reality was all the same
We had infinite variety that never changed
Churches or laws need not to exist
If
Only we allowed our sweet Lord
To reach us through the mist

TURBULENT YEARS
IN CHELSEA

DOCUMENTING LIFE IN THE '70s & '80s

ARNIE JARMAK AND JOSHUA RESNEK

THE
History
PRESS

Published by The History Press
Charleston, SC
www.historypress.com

First published 2020

Manufactured in the United States

ISBN 9781540242549

Library of Congress Control Number: 2019954254

Entering Chelsea, established 1624.

To Andrew P. Quigley for his friendship and love of life and for allowing us to express ourselves as young men.

And to our parents, Ruth and Jerry Jarmak, Sarah and Moses Resnek, who loved and supported us always.

CONTENTS

CLUB CHELSEA

T his is a story about the recent, fateful, "turbulent years" of the small city of Chelsea, Massachusetts, situated just one mile away from the border of the wealthy, thriving city of Boston. It is also the story of an unlikely collaboration between two Jewish boyhood friends from the Boston suburbs and the scrappy survivors, politicos and down-and-out Depression holdovers they encountered in the historic, colonial town established in 1624 during one of its most fraught periods: from the late 1970s through the early 1990s—a brief but consequential time in Chelsea's long history. The two friends, now college-educated men with no marketable skills, improbably started their professional lives as journalists—one a photographer (Arnold Jarmak), the other a writer (Joshua Resnek). This book tells many unknown or forgotten stories of struggle from a tumultuous period in Chelsea's history some forty years ago but also pays tribute to the marginalized, the destitute and the new immigrants—both young and old—who populated the city in a range of street photographs from the spontaneous to the surreptitious to joyfully posed collaborative portraits.

As I grew up privileged in Marblehead, ten miles from Chelsea on Boston's North Shore, Chelsea beckoned me—Joshua Resnek—and my oldest friend, Arnold "Arnie" Jarmak. We escaped Marblehead's beauty, serenity and conservative persona when we came to Chelsea as young men in our twenties, a few years out of college, to work as journalists. Chelsea represented a departure and reprieve from our upbringing. Most of our baby

View from city hall spire.

boomer buddies jumped head-first into the rat race after college. Finding themselves wasn't a desire or an option. We found it difficult to conform. We were always headed in a different direction. We never dreamed of the events we would witness or report on in the small city of Chelsea or that our lifelong collaboration as best friends would continue as a photographer and a writer in the same city working for the same daily newspaper. We became survivors of our white, upper-middle-class upbringing. We traded Marblehead for Chelsea. It turned out to be a good trade.

When we arrived in Chelsea in 1977, the city was locked in a time warp and an ongoing deep and downward socioeconomic spiral. We discovered a disappearing city. It was a kind of perverse Shangri-La. Chelsea's wards and neighborhoods were lined with empty wooden three-decker houses with broken windows and boarded-up doorways. The streets were filled with trash and burned out automobiles. The many churches and synagogues were shuttered, dying institutions. The visage was that of a decadent, hopeless urban mess.

Everything about Chelsea seemed tired and foreboding, rotted and crumbling, as if painted with a dull gray patina except for the people of the city. We could not have known it then, but we were jetting through an extraordinary, irreplaceable, commanding time in our lives. This was our transformative experience, our trip to the moon or the bottom of the sea, to a land quite unlike any other for us. This small city and its people were the stage on which the story of our lives would play out.

Despite having attended respectable, four-year private universities in Pennsylvania and Washington, D.C., we were young men out of control. We had no idea what we were doing professionally or personally. But we became fixtures of sorts in this 1.8-square-mile city in the shadow of Boston, on the northern bank of the Mystic River, during this period we are calling the "Turbulent Years."

From the mid-1970s to the early 1990s, we bore witness to the turbulence of the place from our differing points of view as a photographer and as a writer for the pages of the *Chelsea Record*—the local daily newspaper. We traveled among the well-known and the unknown in all the city's small circles—and loved it. We reported on life in a city where the rubber met the road, where endemic poverty, ignorance, anger, alcoholism, drug addiction, greed and corruption were pervasive forces in nearly every transaction made within its limits.

We became addicted to life in Chelsea—Club Chelsea, we called it. We became well-known throughout the city, initially as reporters and as residents and later as property owners, businessmen, partiers and always as

Last outpost of Washington's army in Chelsea.

Arnie Jarmak with his 8x10 Deardorf camera, vacant lot on Walnut Street, 1978.

guys taking it to the edge, as best friends during an era in our lives now part of a vanishing past. The Chelsea experience made us humble and grateful. It taught us about people—all different kinds of people—about loyalties shared, loyalties broken and loyalties not given.

Through the photographs Arnie Jarmak published and the stories I wrote in the *Chelsea Record* during those years, we earned the respect of the community—politicians, municipal employees, local club members, gamblers and prostitutes; the English and the non-English speakers; blacks, Hispanics and whites; the rich and the poor and the destitute; the Jews, the Catholics and the Russian Orthodox. We especially came to love the characters dressed in rags and dirty clothes, living on the street, eating scraps from trash barrels or dumpsters, crashing in warm hallways or living desperate lives in rooming houses. We came to know them all—and they came to know us.

Not everyone was trapped in Chelsea, and not everyone was dead poor. Many proud old Chelsea families remained. Not everyone moved to the suburbs. We made many friends of young men and women and of people of every age, race and color when we began roaming about the city. The place was vibrant and alive but not prospering. It was welcoming. Everyone knew

Dave, Broadway.

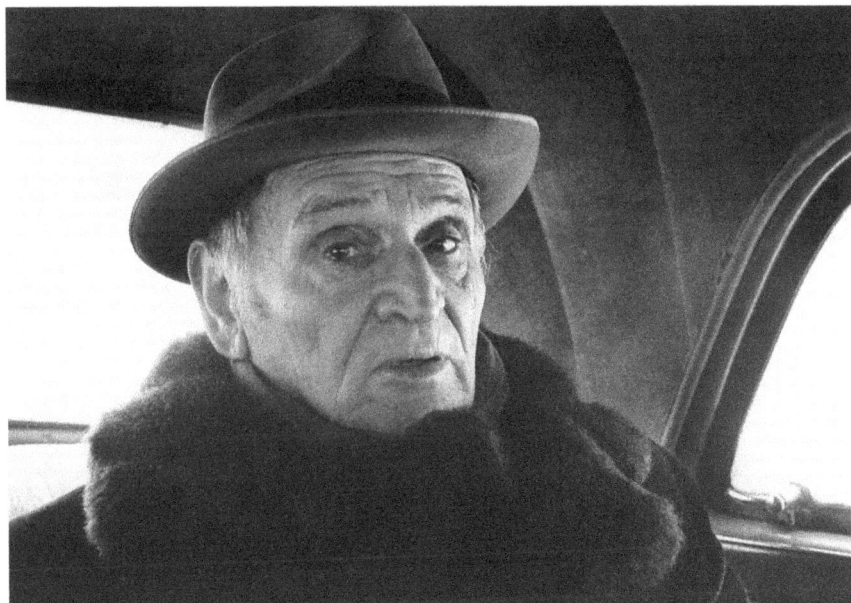

Jack Shore, one of Chelsea's wealthiest longtime business owners, 1984.

everyone else. It was a tight community. People lived on top of one another in one of the most densely populated, dying cities in the nation. People still live here on top of one another.

We stood side by side with Andrew Quigley, publisher of the *Chelsea Record*, and his two sons as loyalists, fighting the good fight to save the city, or at least to give it a new direction and a different, highly personalized look at itself. With the support of Mr. Quigley, as we always called him, we developed our narrative and our take on life, something this book attempts to explain.

What were we thinking, choosing Chelsea's brutal reality as the place we decided to make our home and discover our lives? We remained in Chelsea long after our journalist days ended—as artists of sorts, creators, rebels, builders, takers-apart, fools living out a fool's dream. Experience is the name so many people give to their mistakes is how Oscar Wilde put it. Chelsea might have been our biggest mistake, but then who would we have become in our lives without Chelsea? We were our own lost generation. Now, we are like Proust writing our own *Remembrance of Things Past*. "The sun also ariseth, and the sun goeth down, and hasteth to the place where he arose," as Hemingway wrote in *The Sun Also Rises*.

1

THE QUIGLEYS
AND THE RESNEKS

I n the fall of 1977, I applied for a reporter's position at the *Chelsea Record*, the only daily newspaper in town, owned by Andrew P. Quigley. Quigley had bought the *Record* in the fall of 1976 during a strike by its compositors. The proud old daily was nearly dead when he got it. At that time, Quigley towered as the leading political figure in the city. No one understood the concept of conflict of interest. The Quigley name was the most widely known in the city. His reputation preceded him. His father, Lawrence, was the mayor for many years during the 1920s and 1930s. Andrew Quigley followed in his father's footsteps, serving as mayor, representative and state senator, all before he was twenty-five.

Quigley was a familiar name to me even though I didn't grow up in Chelsea. Chelsea was familiar to me because I spent so much of my time as a youngster there at my father's business in Chelsea Square. (I have always believed I had the best of two worlds: the city of Chelsea and my family home and upbringing in Marblehead.) The Resneks came penniless and unable to speak English from Russia, sailing from Riga on a steamer and landing with their bags of rags and brass pots. They were put up by cousins who had come earlier to the Lower East Side of New York City.

This was 1885. A short time later, my great-grandfather Josiah and my grandfather Louis sailed to Boston, where they briefly lived in the West End—which no longer exists—before moving to Chelsea. The women remained in Kobylnik, Belorussia (Belarus), until the men could be sure of a place to live before coming to America—first New York and then to Chelsea.

Joshua Resnek, age twenty-seven, 1977.

Many cousins remained behind in Kobylnik, too timid, too devoted to the land of their ancestors or too blind to opportunity to make the journey to the New World. Those who remained were all rounded up in 1942 by the Nazis and to a person sent to their deaths at Auschwitz.

In 1898, my grandfather Louis Resnek married Esther Horovitz in Boston. Louis grew up with Esther in Kobylnik, a small town about seventy-five miles

Above: Louis and son David Resnek, Joshua Resnek's grandfather and uncle, in front of Resnek's Kosher Meat Market, circa 1908. *Courtesy Resnek Family Archives.*

Left: Resnek's drugstore in Chelsea Square, the year it closed, 1974. *Courtesy Resnek Family Archives.*

from Minsk on the banks of Lake Narach, where our people had lived for better or worse as oppressed Jews in poverty and indifference for hundreds of years. The Resneks of Chelsea morphed from Russian Orthodox Jewish butchers to educated property owners, numbering themselves among the early well-to-do in the immigrant city by 1925.

Chelsea experienced transformational changes during the four decades between 1890 and 1930. The massive waves of immigration of Irish, Italians, Poles and Russian Jews in the first few decades of the twentieth century started to overwhelm the old-time Protestant Chelsea business and landowners and to create unwanted change. The Protestant churches that dotted the crowded landscape of the burgeoning city were being replaced, their congregations overrun en masse by the construction of synagogues and Catholic churches, which followed the profound demographic changes in the city fueled by immigration.

The greatest alterations to what had been a neat and clean, fairly abundant and all-Protestant Chelsea occurred around the turn of the twentieth century. With the establishment of Catholic churches, and their thousands of faithful followers, came the social and political power that emanated from their growing numbers, then the entrance to the ultimate place, emergence into the Chelsea political arena. Everything political and social in the Chelsea of this era was about exclusion of the newcomers by the old-line Protestants. They watched it coming, the way we can watch a tsunami building before it ushers in a massive flood and washes away all the vestiges of what came before.

It wasn't just the Irish and the Jews dramatically altering the look and feel of turn-of-the-century Chelsea. The Italians, the Polish, the Armenians, the Greeks and smatterings of others—a few Chinese, some Romanians and Bulgarians and a handful of African Americans—all lived together, for better or worse, in the rapidly changing city.

To the utter and complete amazement and frustration of the old-line Chelsea city leaders and church people, these new immigrants practicing different religions, speaking English as a second language and living in housing fit only for them on streets carved out of the former farming community of the 1840s were the rough equivalent of a dehumanizing catastrophe for longtime residents. It was as if Martians by the tens of thousands had invaded Chelsea.

These new residents met derision and hostility from the old-line patrician Chelsea Protestants at city hall or wherever the city's administrative presence was felt—at the library, at the Frost Hospital and in the small retail shops dotting the landscape. These newcomers were not a welcome addition to the old Chelsea families still populating the city and running it with an iron fist.

The early Jews, Irish and Eastern Europeans who arrived in the beginning of the twentieth century were treated the same way the Puerto Rican economic migrants were treated when they came to Chelsea during the 1970s onward. As the city filled with these immigrant waves at the start of the twentieth century, the Jews and the Irish predominated in numbers. In attempting to create lives and incomes for themselves, they used their typical European passion and eye for figuring out how to take over control and manipulate to their own advantage—everything the Protestants held dear to themselves for two centuries. Since colonial times, when Chelsea was still a pastoral community, Protestants owned the city, its land and its means of production.

The Industrial Revolution changed all that. The lazy farm village in the shadow of rising Boston transformed itself from something almost refined created over many, many decades to the exact opposite. Old estates were broken up. Factory housing took their place in the rising industrial city. Single-family residences disappeared, and multifamily housing took their places. Brick sidewalks were paved. Old shade trees were cut down. Everything about the city changed when Man was tossed from the land and sent into factories. Chelsea was always crowded, but now the population was coming to live literally on top of one another.

The Chelsea stove and box factories, tile manufacturers, shipbuilders and shoe companies came to be filled mainly by Irish employees mostly from the mass exodus during the Great Famine from County Cork. The greatest number of Irish came nearer to the end of the nineteenth century, finding work, living with relatives, building Catholic churches and forming the beginnings of parish life. From parish life came a logical extension—the political arm that gave the Irish a budding sense of belonging and of wanting to control their new environment. Oddly enough, the first two places the Irish found employment in the city were the police and fire departments. The first Irish police officers and firefighters appear on the city payroll in the late 1880s. The Irish became the beat cops like those depicted in movies romanticizing the Victorian era. The early Irish cops kept the peace in the changing city. They were tough, not particularly liberal, but savvy in the ways of the new land. The same is true for the firefighters corralling horse-driven pumpers, smokestacks churning, charging down Broadway or Everett Avenue responding to an alarm.

The Jews set up shop on Second Street, where they collected rags and scraps of steel and sold it like commodities to manufacturers. They set up small fish stores and varieties and tailor shops on Arlington Street, which was cobblestoned and could serve today as a movie set depicting a turn-of-the-century city fueled by European immigration.

Naturally, the Jews built synagogues, more than a dozen of them by 1910. Like the Irish, their political aspirations gained shape and form at brotherhood meetings with those already succeeding in the new land.

Until the Great Fire of 1908, Chelsea remained a Protestant kingdom—a kingdom in decline but a kingdom nevertheless worth maintaining control over. Chelsea was owned, lock, stock and barrel, by old Protestant families and businesses or interests. Their kingdom fell into decline when it was slowly upended by the upstart Jews and Irish pushing their way into the life and times of the small city. The Protestants would not let go. The newcomers were a distasteful, foreign addition to a city the Protestants believed was beautiful and even historic, given its place in early American history.

The Protestants couldn't believe how the city was changing, as best described in the only modern history of Chelsea, *The Burning of Chelsea* (https://lccn.loc.gov/08019884), written in 1908 after the first massive fire that same year by Walter Merriam Pratt (1880–1973). "It's so sad. You wouldn't recognize the place from 20 years ago. It's being ruined," Pratt writes in a letter to a friend.

General George Washington visited here during the Revolutionary War on several occasions when a part of the Continental army was garrisoned in Washington Park in what is today the neighborhood of Prattville. In fact, he dined with the Pratts, members of Chelsea's oldest family, who settled here in the 1630s and who were here when the city burned in 1908 and until the 1930s, when the old Pratt House was ripped down before it fell to the ground.

Abraham Lincoln came to Chelsea in 1848 and spoke at Gerrish Hall in Chelsea Square. He gave a Whig stump speech when he was a congressman. It is impossible to imagine that this American Jesus had only seventeen years to live when he visited here. Lincoln's visit to Chelsea proved its importance as a political hotbed even during this relatively early period in its development. He almost certainly dined with the Fay, Wilkerson, Stebbins, Gerrish and Nichols families—all prominent, old Chelsea people who were the leaders at that time.

The Great Fire of 1908 devastated the city on a windswept Palm Sunday. Nearly all the city's grand public buildings burned to the ground, including the Fitz Library with the city's meticulously kept handwritten records dating back to the 1600s. Nearly all the city's shade trees on its major streets and thoroughfares were burned to a crisp. The fire burned so hard and so hot that granite curbstones crumbled into dust. The kingdom suffered its seminal loss that day in April. Old Chelsea was swept away.

What journalists found when they came to Chelsea to report on the fire from all over the United States were about ten thousand poverty-stricken, struggling immigrant Jews and Irish, in shock, living in the streets and squares and inside their churches and synagogues for the first few days afterward. The grand old homes of the landed gentry, the early families and

Left: Abraham Lincoln visited Chelsea, Gerrish Hall, Chelsea Square.

Below: Archival photo of 1908 Chelsea Fire. *Courtesy Chelsea Library Digital Collections.*

the great early industrialists that lined Bellingham Hill from the bottom of Bellingham Square to the top of Bellingham Street had been reduced to piles of rubble and sent to the far reaches of the earth as ash and dust. Out of this catastrophe rose a new city with the emblem of it, Chelsea City Hall, designed after Independence Hall in Philadelphia and standing majestically and strategically at the center of the city.

The tremendous growth caused by European immigration during the 1890s helped to alter and reshape the face of the city. World War I made many Chelsea merchant families rich. Even the general population benefited from the full employment the war brought. The Resneks were like other early Jewish immigrant families headed by strong, ambitious, forward-thinking men and women who came from Russia and Poland, who became knowing in the ways of the new land and accumulated small fortunes. They grew large families, sent their kids to college and enjoyed everything America had to offer while remaining in Chelsea to share in the family's new wealth and status. To these men and women with vigor and ambition, Chelsea was a great and wonderful place. It was a world unto itself with Boston less than a mile away.

Chelsea's name and its history, as such, date back to the early seventeenth century. By the time of the outbreak of the Revolutionary War, Beacon Hill and Bunker Hill had been stripped bare of trees. The land had been skinned as cleanly as a fish of its scales. Modern Boston grew with speed and an indifference to space or to common sense. The rush was to build, to grow, to prosper. Modern Chelsea began to take shape and form. Roads and streets were cut, buildings rose in clusters, spread into new neighborhoods and culminated with a large population of people burning tremendous amounts of wood. The British troops stationed in nearby Charlestown ravaged the food supplies of the Sagamore Indians in Chelsea from time to time. General George Washington garrisoned the northern wing of the Continental army in Prattville, in the park named after him. Washington Avenue is also named for him.

At the time of the Revolutionary War, about 450 people lived in Chelsea, mostly on farms, earning their livings as farmers. By 1800, 160 years since the first European settlement in Chelsea, the Sagamore were nearly extinct and their outposts in the lush marshlands spreading north had almost completely disappeared. Chelsea grew slowly, first as a farmland type of appurtenance to Boston, only one mile away, and gradually into an industrial laboratory. With the advent of the steam engine and the rise of the Industrial Revolution, Chelsea's three major farms—the Shurtleff,

Williams and Cary farms—were sold, their lands subdivided into smaller parcels available for sale. By 1848, the entire area known today as Chelsea was beginning to sprawl with industry and small factories, coal storage depots and even some shipbuilding on the shore and smaller manufacturers of stoves and boxes. Church life provided government and structure, education and charity. The population had exploded to 5,300. At the time of the Civil War, the population stood at 14,000. In 1885, when my great-grandfather Josiah Resnek came to Chelsea from Russia, more than 25,000 residents were churning inside this 1.8-square-mile rising American "metropolis."

Nothing in its three-hundred-plus-year history affected Chelsea so greatly as the Industrial Revolution. What began with a trickle during the Civil War led to the mass immigration to Boston and to Chelsea from Europe of tens of thousands of Irish and Jews, Poles and Italians fleeing abject poverty and religious discrimination for the Promise of America—and for the chance to work behind machines and to get paid. Horrible and unsafe working conditions abounded in Chelsea's early factories and manufacturing plants. Children and adults lost their fingers and hands. Other workers during this early industrial period became poisoned. The land lost every measure of its purity in this unbridled race for progress and for profits. By 1900, Chelsea's land base was largely polluted. In some parts of the city, once a romantic farm and sailing mecca, a flower couldn't be grown because the land was too polluted.

The dramatic decades of growth and consolidation between 1885 and 1925 marked Chelsea's fantasyland years. By the end of the nineteenth century, developers of the city divided Chelsea into neat wards, lined with parallel streets with multiunit homes to house all the thousands of laborers needed to operate the machines behind which men, women and children worked inside its factories. A town government had risen to tax early residents and property owners and, especially, the spate of businesses that had changed the face of the place. Small city developers built new housing stock.

The Roaring Twenties produced a steep rise in the value of Chelsea's housing stock, in the depth and growing strength of its vastly expanded business community, and brought to a righteous boil its many and varied social and religious institutions. The city's population reached almost fifty thousand. It became an immigrant empire where English was a second language, as it is today. Cars, transit buses and trucks clogged the city's streets. Business and unbridled commerce marked the city's emergence as a substantial place of its own in the shadow of Boston.

Following an explosive expansion of business and commerce during the First World War, nearly every available open space from the Chelsea line down to the Mystic River and west to the Medford border was covered by mountains of coal or by oil tanks. Second Street from Chelsea Square to the Everett line became inhabited mostly by the junkers and the rag shops—recyclers of steel and other metals and rags, who plied their products out of filthy yards and shops lining the length of Second Street from Everett and the Revere Beach Parkway to Chelsea. Unbeknownst to its rag and scrap-metal merchants, Chelsea became one of the nation's first recycling centers.

Several dozen manufacturers abounded along the front of the Chelsea River, also known as Chelsea Creek. The Broadway business district served the entire city the way shopping centers miles away would nearly destroy it many years later. The city government improved infrastructure. Police and fire services grew with the population—which continued to increase with waves of immigrants until the nation shut off immigration during the Red Scare in the early 1920s. The quintessentially American society of an immigrant "melting pot" grew and prospered in the Chelsea of this extraordinary era.

From the beginning of the Resneks' time in Chelsea, my family lived on Beacon Street, almost on the harbor, in a small apartment in a red brick bow front building. The family butcher store operated out of a basement space in a small apartment house on Tremont Street, a stone's throw from today's oil depot at the end of Lower Broadway. That building still stands. After the Great Chelsea Fire of 1908, the Resneks were one of the first families to rebuild on Williams Street. They lived in a long row of red brick three-story, three-family homes that lined the street and worked in a first-floor business they named Resnek's Kosher Meat Market, where the Chelsea District Court House stands today. In the early years after the Great Fire, the Quigleys lived around the corner from the Resneks at the Imperial Building on Lower Broadway.

The Quigleys were haberdashers, working out of a storefront in Chelsea Square they named Quigley and Noone. Early on, from the turn of the twentieth century, the Quigleys were the city's most noted Irish political family from County Cork. They arrived in Chelsea about the same time as the Resneks, although the Lawlors, with whom the Quigleys intermarried in the Old World before coming to America, arrived in Chelsea in 1848 at the height of the great Irish Famine, which coincided with the birth of the Industrial Revolution. The Irish found jobs as police officers and city workers, truck drivers and hard laborers who ended up working behind machines for

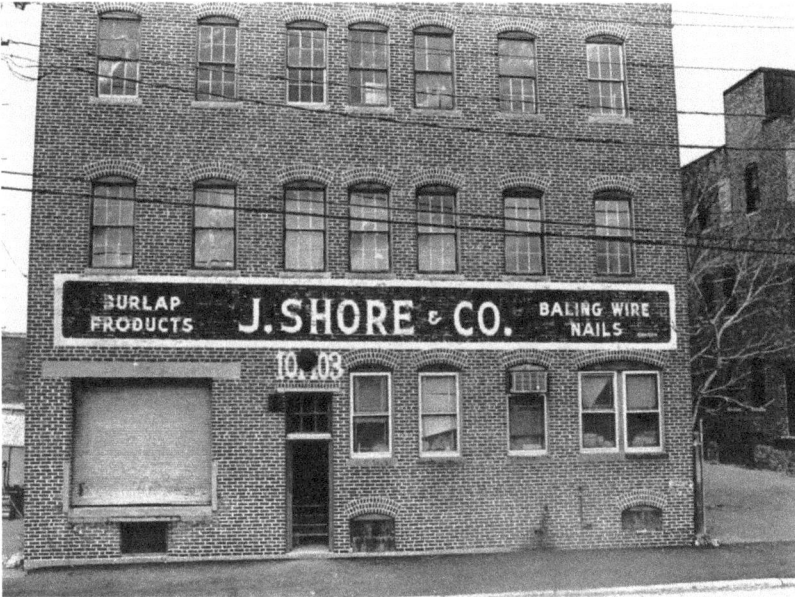

Above: J. Shore & Co. storefront, Second Street.

Left: 1890s façade of the Chelsea Police Station and Courthouse.

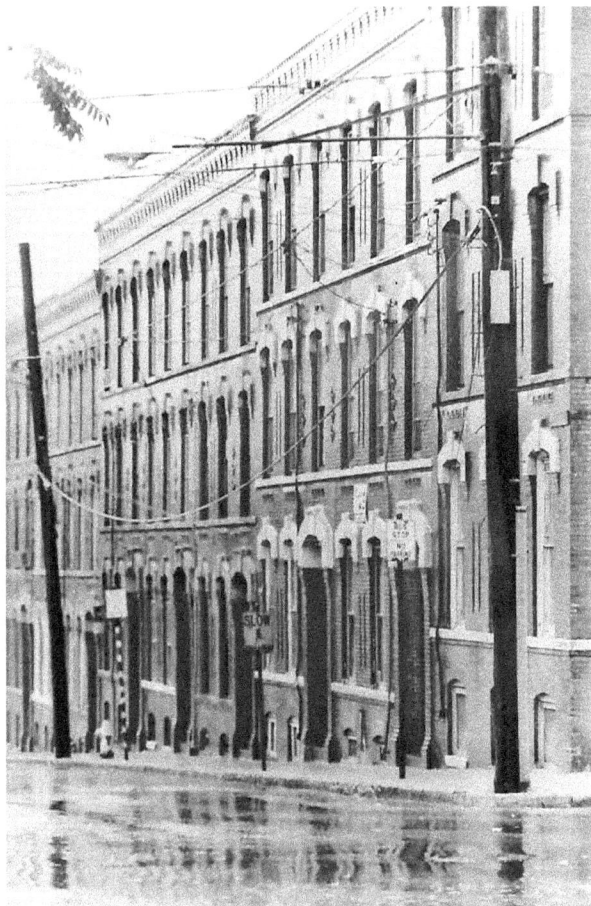

Beacon Street
"brownstones."

box manufacturers or stove makers, in businesses mostly owned by old-time Chelsea Protestant families who held quiet disdain for the newcomers.

Lawrence Quigley rose to lead the Irish and the Jews of Chelsea at the height of their immigrant struggle. He would represent every group willing to back him as long they and their families returned the favors he got them with their votes. He spoke Gaelic. He learned Yiddish. He had the upper-dog's concern for the underdog. Lawrence Quigley ruled Chelsea City Hall. Through the power of his personality, Quigley came to own city hall. He was a true orator: the most commanding city leader with a golden tongue and an understanding of its history. He was a generous and engaging presence at city hall and throughout Chelsea. Lawrence Quigley was the ultimate Roosevelt New Deal Democrat. He knew how to wow his crowd. The working-class Jews, almost twenty thousand strong in the city by the 1920s, elected him every two years. Their vote made the whole difference—even when a Jewish candidate ran, Quigley, the Irishman, almost always won with the Jewish vote out of its Ward 2 stronghold. He ennobled city employees. He praised the common man and supported the working poor. On Thanksgiving, he gave out turkeys to those who couldn't afford them. At Christmas, he did the same. If you couldn't afford to bury your dead, Quigley could be relied on.

An election for mayor in the early 1920s produced one of Mayor Quigley's most memorable moments that aroused his Jewish supporters. The interaction between two candidates, the Jew and the Irishman, appearing in debate before an entirely Jewish crowd, speaks more about Quigley's hubris than it does about his opponent's over-qualifications. Colonel Clarence Richmond was a lawyer, a colonel in the U.S. Army, a battlefield veteran of the First World War and from one of the oldest and most distinguished Jewish families in the city. Mayor Quigley and Colonel Richmond were in a neck-to-neck battle for the corner office. A debate between the two candidates was held at the Williams School auditorium. The Williams School sat in the middle of Jewish Chelsea, the teeming Ward 2 district with dozens of cobblestone streets, small shops, drugstores, corner varieties, a few restaurants (delis), three-decker homes, larger apartment houses and a spate of synagogues.

Perhaps two thousand voters, mostly Jews, seated and standing on top of one another, cheered wildly as the candidates came out for a bow on the stage. The debate got underway. It had gone on for about a half hour when Richmond reached his high point. Harvard-educated Richmond, tall and lean and dressed in a conservative wool pin-stripe three-piece suit, spoke eloquently about his rival to his people, the Jews he expected would vote for him. It went something like this, according to my late father, Moses Resnek.

Richmond asked Mayor Quigley about his sincerity. "Boss Quigley will tell you he is a good friend of the Jewish people. He really isn't a friend of the Jewish people. Ask him how many Jews he's hired to work for the city as police or firefighters? Ask him why there isn't a single Jewish firefighter or police officer." The crowd cheered Colonel Richmond.

Now came to the stage Mayor Quigley wearing his top hat, black tuxedo tails, black bow tie and a crisp triple white shirt with golden cufflinks. "There's Quigley," many in the crowd whispered in broken English to one another as he stood before them. He looked out at the crowd, first-generation immigrant Jews living and working in the most crowded ward in the city dressed in their work clothes, many sporting long white beards or wearing yarmulkes. Mayor Quigley raised the microphone to his mouth. He pointed to his opponent Colonel Richmond deferentially with a bow.

"My good friend Clarence Richmond has told you I am not a friend of the Jewish people." The Robin Hood of modern Chelsea, the Irish mayor stealing from the rich to give to the poor, looked out upon his people. "Let me ask you this. What Jewish mother and father in this crowd raises their son to be a firefighter or police officer? No, you good people work hard so your children can go to college and become doctors, lawyers and accountants. That's why I've never appointed a Jewish fireman or policeman." The crowd roared for Mayor Quigley. He won the election of 1920 with the biggest plurality in his career.

During the Jewish High Holidays in September, Mayor Quigley walked the streets of Chelsea in his tuxedo, tipping his top hat, stopping to speak to Jewish families in Yiddish, walking from one to another of the thirteen synagogues situated throughout the city—as he knew they wouldn't drive—in a dramatic and personal show of political acumen and Irish-style tribalism. Today, all such remembrances are anecdotal. Nothing appeared about his actions in the *Chelsea Record* of this era. No story. No photographs. What a person he must have been, and what a time that was in the history of the small city.

My grandfather Louis Resnek was one of the largest property owners in the city when Lawrence Quigley came to power. Their paths crossed many times during the great years of growth and many more times as everything went the other way. The coming of the Great Depression first stunted and then stopped all growth in Chelsea as it wore on. It sucked hope out of the people. The unbridled growth and optimism of the Roaring Twenties became a postscript nearly overnight to this new and destructive period, which would affect the city for decades to come.

My grandfather put my father and his brother George, my uncle, into business. He opened Resnek's Drug Store for them in 1926 in the Exchange Building, which he bought in 1912. Located at the corner of Broadway and Cross Street, the Exchange Building anchored the block he owned in Chelsea Square. On the second floor, my uncle David kept his law office, although he never practiced law. My aunt Dorothy graduated from Jackson College, the all-women's college, now part of Tufts University. All the Resneks lived a charmed life in Chelsea as young adults.

Resnek's Drug Store, with its long marble fountain and handmade oak cabinets, tile floor and ornate, punched tin ceiling—with my grandfather, my father and uncles presiding—was the place where official Chelsea collected

Chelsea Square, summer.

every morning: lawyers, judges, property owners, city employees and nearly every family living in or within the Chelsea Square nexus. It was a bit like the corner drugstores brought to life in Sinclair Lewis's 1922 masterpiece *Babbitt*, which satirizes American life as its grandest era got underway.

During the Depression, the Resneks and the Quigleys didn't change their lifestyles. They didn't have to. They remained true to their upbringings as humble, modest, educated people who never discriminated against others, as that would have been like discriminating against themselves. They inevitably, irrevocably, never forgot the European diaspora from which they came—it brought them to America. My grandfather fled the Russian Empire's poverty and its anti-Semitism; Lawrence Quigley's Irish ancestors were nearly starved to death by absentee British landowners during the Great Irish Famine of the late 1840s.

How the nation went from soaring optimism to darkness and depression during the economic catastrophe is the stuff of our national history. In Chelsea, during the height of the Depression in 1935, with thousands out of work in the city, so many homes being foreclosed on and no social welfare programs in place to take the rough edge off the growing disaster, Mayor Quigley appointed my grandfather to the Chelsea Stadium Commission. It was the largest WPA (Works Progress Administration) building project in

CHELSEA MEMORIAL STADIUM COMMISSION
1934-1935

Chelsea Memorial Stadium Committee, 1934–35, including Lawrence Quigley (*top center*) and Louis Resnek (*top right*). *Courtesy of Joshua Resnek.*

the city. About five thousand Chelsea men were employed on and off at the project site on Everett Avenue for more than two years. Thousands of destitute Chelsea families about to lose their homes welcomed the project. Under my grandfather's stern edict, every contract for cement, steel, wood and landscaping or fencing used to construct and to finish the stadium and its playing field was given to the lowest bidder. The neediest were hired first; first-generation Irish, Poles, Italians and Jews built the stadium.

The opening of Chelsea Memorial Stadium in 1937 brought out a massive crowd of dignitaries, one hundred military leaders and leaders from around the nation and the state in tuxedos and top hats, flags flying and bands playing, all celebrating its completion as though the Roman Colosseum had opened its gates for the games to begin. Thousands of Chelsea residents attended as well. Mayor Quigley provided free refreshments for everyone who came. The mayor delivered a stirring speech in his tuxedo and top hat. My grandfather and his many colleagues in government in Chelsea listened intently. Quigley finished with a line reported in the *Chelsea Record*: "Let us never forget those who gave their lives in the First World War so we might be here today dedicating this great monument to their sacrifice." When the cheering stopped that day, the Great Depression began anew and with a vengeance. That was 1937.

Triple-deckers and city hall spire.

The stadium no longer exists. What remains today is an artificial grass football field behind the Chelsea High School. The stadium and its massive cement and steel stands capable of seating ten thousand were demolished and carted away. All that remains of that great monument to the First World War dead is a giant brass plaque memorializing Gold Star mothers who lost their sons during the war. It is mounted on a small brick wall where cars park to remind those of what had come before. Almost no one looks at it.

Fast-forward to 1977. Chelsea was not a place where people like me—college graduates from better homes who enjoyed the ease of upper-middle-class suburban American life—desired to be in the 1970s. Chelsea was shunned by the outside world, which looked on it as a place where there was darkness, poverty, corruption, violence and hopelessness. There was all of this—but there was more. There was mystery and drama, love and hate, miracles and disasters. I was twenty-seven years old and at the end of my first marriage when I arrived in Chelsea in 1977. I was looking at options, trying to figure out what to do as a next step.

The way of life in Chelsea was dominated by a corrupt, dysfunctional city government, a system of governing that resembled and mimicked something from decades before—a retrograde patriarchal society amid the Hippie Generation. Everyone was welcome to come and go from Chelsea, but the shadow of city hall remained prominent. City hall was a hard place to break into, but once penetrated, it became a place you felt you could own. At the same time, the place was a mess. It was going down.

My college degree in history prepared me for nothing that I was able to immediately monetize. My personal journey to find something meaningful to do with my life began after college. This led me and my best friend to Chelsea from Brookline, where I had been living in a rent-free apartment building my family gave to me to manage in 1972. I earned meager money as a freelance writer while trying to secure full-time employment as a writer or reporter; nothing was more important or quite so impossible for me then. In September 1975, the *New York Times* op-ed page featured a full-page piece I wrote about a ride through Brooklyn in my then-father-in-law's Cadillac— and a look at the poverty and the decadence of New York City. I was on my way. I wrote freelance sports features for the *Lynn Item* and the *Beverly Times*.

Arnie Jarmak graduated from Marblehead High School in 1967 and, like me, with me, wandered far away from our upbringings when we went out into the world to experience our lives. He, too, was changed by the 1968 social revolution. He attended Lehigh University in Pennsylvania. His college experience was a mirror image of my own, feeding our neediness, denying us the easy way out. He was destined to be a photographer. He didn't know this any more than I knew I would be a reporter when we graduated from college.

A glimmer of hope appeared when Andrew Quigley purchased the *Chelsea Record*. The small daily newspaper was on strike. No one in their right mind would buy it. For Quigley, owning the newspaper was a dream come true, something that would never have been allowed for an Irishman or a Jew by its Protestant owners unless for the economic catastrophe the city was suffering. The newspaper was struggling. It lost half its circulation between 1950 and 1976. Most of its longtime employees had been laid off. My father suggested I get in touch with Quigley. "Tell Andrew who you are and who your grandfather was," my father told me. This was sage advice.

It bears repeating that no one with any common sense wanted to be in Chelsea, move to Chelsea or write for the *Chelsea Record*—much less be the photographer for the newspaper. In 1977, longtime residents were leaving Chelsea, abandoning the city in droves. The only newcomers were poverty-stricken, illiterate, Spanish-speaking Puerto Ricans largely shunned and looked down on by the Anglo population and excluded overtly from the government that ran the city. Most people living outside the city considered Chelsea a dump. Suburbanites ridiculed the place. Newspaper

Andrew Quigley at the *Chelsea Record* offices, 1980.

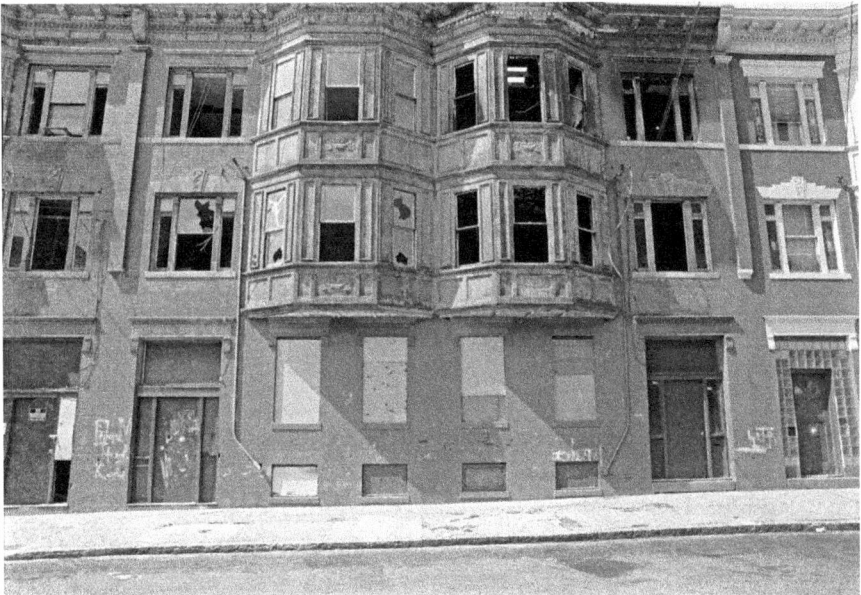

Abandoned buildings, Walnut Street.

and television news stories highlighting drug addiction, poverty, illegal gaming and the host of urban ills alive and well in Chelsea muddied its name and colored a desperate picture of life in the city. Old families were fleeing Chelsea for the suburbs.

I called Quigley. He was pleasant enough. He didn't give away his hand. He knew who I was. "Louie's grandson?" he asked. "Yes. Yes," I replied. We set up an appointment. He told me to come in to meet with him the following day. I first met Mr. Quigley in his cluttered first-floor office on Fourth Street. These had been the offices of the *Chelsea Record* since its founding in 1898. He sat behind a large antique oak roll-top desk filled with papers and books that rested atop a gorgeous Oriental rug. The books had titles like *The Burning of Chelsea* or *The History of Chelsea*, and there were many smaller Victorian volumes, collections of photographs of Chelsea in the 1880s and 1890s. The walls were covered with fine art, beautiful nineteenth-century oil paintings and twentieth-century impressionistic works created by major Boston artists. A framed photograph of Mr. Quigley in tennis whites, holding a racket and posing with a young Jack Kennedy standing next to him in Palm Beach right after the war was signed, "To my good friend, Andrew." Rolled up oriental rugs were everywhere. It was an astonishing office to walk into—and to think, I was in Chelsea!

Mr. Quigley had a large head with all-seeing eyes. He was a bit overweight and unkempt, balding, totally out of shape. He looked imposing, leaning back in a tall black leather chair, his hands clasped behind his head, his elbows out from side to side. He wore wrinkled khaki pants, a nondescript shirt and dirty old white tennis sneakers—not high tops. He was somewhere in his late forties and absolutely delighted to be the publisher and editor of the *Chelsea Record*. He held a copy of it in his hand. "Tisn't much. But tis my own," he said.

He rose to meet me. We shook hands. "Please, sit down" he said with grace and charm pointing to an old oak and leather chair. "It is such a pleasure to meet so handsome a specimen of a such a prominent former Chelsea family," he said. I had not in all my years of living in Marblehead heard such a learned, sarcastic, yet genuine voice welcoming me. This was the beginning of what would turn out to be a long run.

For the next hour, we talked about our connection to Chelsea. He spoke of his legendary father. I told him how I knew of him, how my father and uncles always referred to him as a strong city hall boss and a friend to the Jewish people. I spoke about my grandfather, the successful Chelsea real estate man and property owner. He told me how well he knew him. It was like old home week. He said he knew the Resnek family home on Tudor Street, the stately Victorian across from the old high school where my grandfather moved the family in 1916. He recalled his father appointing my grandfather to the Stadium Commission. He recalled trying to buy the Italian marble fountain from my father and uncle when they were closing down Resnek's Drug Store in Chelsea Square after a nearly fifty-year run in 1973. "Quigley, the fountain isn't for sale. We'll take care of it," he said my uncle told him. "I was so disappointed," he added. This was typical Resnek disinterest in the outside world trying to come into theirs.

Quigley described Chelsea, its history, its ups and downs, with finesse and expertise. "The city has changed since my father was mayor," he said. "Since I was mayor, the city has lost a huge part of its population, maybe twenty thousand people, including its best families. The Tobin Bridge killed us. Absentee landlords are destroying the place. Everything is falling apart. City hall still controls the city, but even that is failing," he added.

"The *Chelsea Record*," he continued, "remains the voice of the city. We can bring this place back if we work hard at it. Everyone in Chelsea reads the *Record*." "You see this?" he asked me. He pointed to the logo on the front page of the newspaper. "Our readers are our friends."

We discussed how the *Chelsea Record* had always been a part of the lives of Chelsea people and former Chelsea people no matter where they moved. The old and yellowed copies of the *Record*—with pictures and stories about my grandfather or my father or the stadium and the drugstore—were always a part of my childhood, stacked neatly in a corner of my father's study in our home in Marblehead. This didn't mean much to my buddies from Marblehead, but it meant so much to me, even to this day. Decadent, crumbling, ugly old Chelsea was where we came from. I always loved the place and felt a part of it. "I am so sorry you didn't have the advantage of growing up here," Quigley joked. For many years to come, when a Chelsea person I didn't know asked me if I grew up in Chelsea, I did a Quigley. "I didn't have the advantage of growing up in Chelsea," I'd answer. "I grew up in Marblehead."

I wanted a job as a reporter, I told Quigley. I told him I'd work seven days a week, that I'd become the eyes and ears of the *Chelsea Record*. He was kind enough to listen discretely. He seemed interested. He'd have to pay me, I said, but in reality I would have paid him for the opportunity. After an hour, the conversation ended with a phone call that Quigley needed to take. He motioned with his hand for me to leave. "Call me next week," Quigley said. He gave me a smile and a friendly wave as I walked out the door.

Old woman on her back porch, Ward 1.

Doorway No. 44.

American La France ladder truck on Broadway.

I stood on the sidewalk outside the office on Fourth Street after the meeting. I was elated. What a meeting it had been. Didn't matter the walking wounded of American society passed by me as I stood there outside the *Chelsea Record* office. A woman limping with each suffering step pushed a grocery cart. An older, happier drunk said hello to me before raising a bottle of cheap wine to his mouth and gulping it down. An old American La France fire engine from another era, dented and beaten, raced by. Two firefighters sat in the front seat and two hung on to steel posts at the rear of clanking, rusting bucket of bolts, its siren blaring and a single revolving red light spinning at the top of the windshield. An old, black late-1950s Chevrolet police car followed. I watched a crowd collect down the street, where people were being taken away by the police. Wow, I thought.

The fire burning inside could not have been brighter for me. Mr. Quigley's manner, his body language, everything about him and how he spoke with me about our past and the connections between our families' social and political connections gave me hope. Next week couldn't come soon enough.

One week to the day we met, I called Mr. Quigley as instructed at the *Chelsea Record*. "Hi, Mr. Quigley. This is Josh Resnek. You told me to give you a call." "Who is this?" Mr. Quigley replied. The smooth but puzzled voice of the *Chelsea Record* publisher was never more apparent. "Have we spoken before?" he asked. His response startled me. I repeated myself. "This is Josh Resnek. We met last week." "Who?" he repeated. "Josh Resnek. Louis Resnek's grandson. My father owned the drugstore." Like what the f***, I said to myself. Mr. Quigley mumbled a bit. He seemed incoherent. My optimism about this call sank. A moment passed. Then he came out of it: "Of course I remember speaking with you," he said, having a nice laugh for himself. "Come in early tomorrow. You're hired."

Two weeks after Mr. Quigley put me to work, he hired twenty-eight-year-old Arnold Jarmak to be the full-time staff photographer. Enter Arnie into the life and times of the city of Chelsea, Massachusetts. My lifelong friend moved to Chelsea with a Nikon 35mm camera strung around his neck. He was ready for this. He had prepared. The city and its people were about to become his best subject. Arnie packed his things into his Subaru. With his girlfriend Jan he left the farm he was living on in Durham, New Hampshire, where he was a graduate student at the University of New Hampshire. He drove down to Chelsea, to the east end of Broadway, across from the oil farm, to number 26, where Mr. Quigley had given me an apartment on the first floor in the last house on Broadway, Gardner House, the second-oldest home in Chelsea, built in 1807. Arnie moved his books and his prized cameras into the second-floor apartment. We were on our way.

We were wild with excitement. We had both gotten full-time jobs at a daily newspaper. Arnie's parents and my parents all frowned. Couldn't we do something more useful with our lives than work for Mr. Quigley as a photographer and writer for the small *Chelsea Record*? Couldn't we conform? How could we go from Marblehead to Chelsea when everyone in their right mind was going in the opposite direction? "Did we send you to college to end up living and working in Chelsea?" they seemed to say. In moving to Chelsea and pursuing our dreams, we proved to each other we weren't giving up starting out. We weren't selling our souls. We weren't spitting on our own faces, as Ayn Rand writes of life in her introduction to *The Fountainhead*.

We were best friends about to make beautiful, mesmerizing music for ourselves. We were just taking off in our lives, doing what we wanted, freed somehow in our minds having arrived in Chelsea, finding freedom for ourselves, feeling the power that freedom can bring to oneself. Chelsea held her hand out to us. We grabbed it. She flirted with us and flaunted herself.

Laundry, Ward 3.

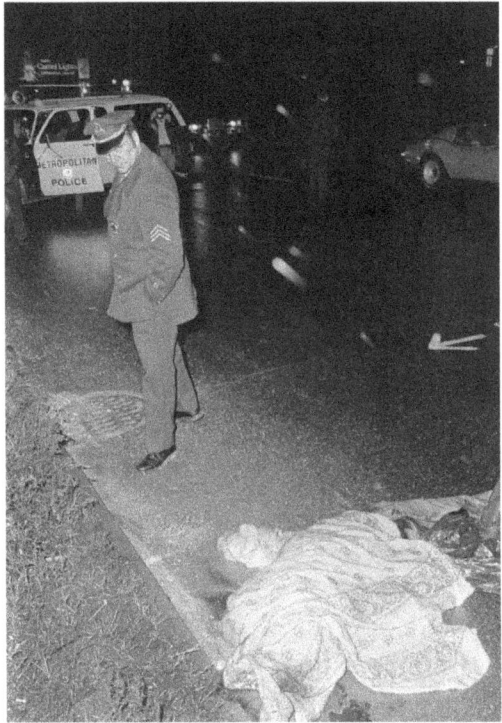

Death on Route 1, 1982.

We became so deeply attracted to her that we couldn't let go, not for a long, long time to come—not ever, really.

Arnie was hired to run the graphic camera in the *Chelsea Record* print shop in order to justify his salary as a photographer. The only reason he was there was to take photographs. He replaced Phil Reddin, who had been charging the *Chelsea Record* $7.50 per print. Arnie offered to do it for $5.00. That was the last time Phil Reddin ever took a picture for the *Chelsea Record*. It appealed to Stephen Quigley, one of Mr. Quigley's two sons, who was responsible for paying the bills. We would have done it for free. We would have paid $500.00—not that we had any money. The money didn't matter; that's why we were in Chelsea. We had a vehicle for self-expression. It was so powerful; it was elegiac. For us at that time, and for many years, the money wasn't everything. What mattered was that we were doing what we loved to do, working for a newspaper, while trying to figure out what we were doing as journalists. There was no other newspaper that would even consider giving us jobs.

We both developed a close relationship with Mr. Quigley. He saw what we saw. He enjoyed what we enjoyed. He believed he could bring back

Harry Siegel portraits of Arnie Jarmak with cameras and portrait with Andrew Quigley and Josh Resnek (*far right*), 1977.

the power of the *Chelsea Record*—and the city with it—with his pen, and he did. He allowed us the freedom to cover what we wanted, to write and photograph to our hearts' content. He allowed us to use this power every day. Quigley's passion for the newspaper was our example. We shared it with him. He loved us for it. We came to love the *Chelsea Record*.

Mr. Quigley also hired Arnie as a carpenter to build a darkroom to house, and then to run, a process camera for the *Chelsea Record*'s new Harris offset press. The entire affair was a hassle. At the time, Mr. Quigley was pressed for cash. Everything was being done on a shoestring, shot from the hip, to get the show on the road. Arnie was good with his hands. He had trained with carpenters in his father's successful school furniture business. He knew how to build. He didn't want to be running the *Chelsea Record*'s process camera. Being the *Chelsea Record*'s photographer was dependent on him running the camera. One didn't go without the other. By default, he became the *Chelsea Record*'s full-time photographer. He would spend one year of his life in that darkroom behind that process camera while also trying to be a daily newspaper photographer before Mr. Quigley hired someone else to run the process camera for the printing business that was an offshoot of the newspaper.

Classic Chelsea three-decker tenements.

Before he moved to Chelsea, Arnie was not as acquainted with it as I was. Like many suburbanites, he passed over Chelsea on the Tobin Bridge numerous times with his parents and looked down on it as the car headed to Boston. He saw up close the distressed living conditions of wooden and brick three-decker tenements, roofs in need of repair with crumbling chimneys and piles of scattered bricks spread atop like broken branches fallen from dying trees. He never got off the bridge and drove into the city when he was a young man. Why would he? Why would anyone? What little he knew about Chelsea came from me and from Ralph Sevinor, a childhood friend from an old Chelsea family. The talk among us was inevitably, always about Chelsea.

Arnie's Chelsea connection is his mother's great-grandfather Jeremiah Wentworth, who moved to Chelsea in 1846 from Maine. The Wentworths came to America in 1630. Jeremiah's grandfather Moses fought in the Revolutionary War. His uncle John served on the USS *Constitution* as a seaman in two major naval engagements, the Battles of Java and Guerriere.

Arnie owed much of his heart and soul to his mother, Ruth. She grew up in humble circumstances in Beachmont, a neighborhood in nearby Revere, where her Irish father, Patrick Shanahan, drove a Metropolitan District Commission truck for twenty-five years on Revere Beach. Her mother, Esther Miller, was a Polish Jew who grew up from age nine in the west end of Boston. The Shanahans came to Boston in the 1840s during the Irish potato famine. Arnie's great-great-grandfather Daniel Shanahan served in the Union army in the Civil War and died in the service of his country in North Carolina. The Shanahans lived in the west end of Boston and had a moving company, first with a horse and wagon and then a truck.

Arnie's mother became an oil painter and a bit of a musician. With her support and urging, Arnie was able to search out his dreams. Arnie's mother met and married his father, Jerry Jarmak, shortly before he was shipped out to Europe during the Second World War. His father attained the rank of captain. He traveled across Europe with the U.S. Air Force as the commanding officer of an ordinance company serving in England, France and Germany. Throughout his childhood and into adulthood, Arnie felt the conflicting influences of his Irish-Jewish mother and his Ukrainian Jewish father.

Jerry Jarmak, Arnie's father, grew up in Ansonia, Connecticut. His father, Aaron, came to the United States from Ukraine in 1906 through Ellis Island. Aaron became a successful merchant and real estate owner, but the early death of both parents—first his mother, Mary, in 1916, when Jerry was five, and then his father, Aaron, in 1926, when Jerry was thirteen—led to hard times. The family of eight children was raised by a stepmother, and by 1934, they were evicted from the family home in the middle of the Great Depression. His family lost everything. After serving in the war, Jerry started the Jarmak Corporation, which he built into a successful construction and sales company helping to build schools and hospitals and universities throughout New England. He did not want his family to go through what he had as a young boy growing up. It was his hope that Arnie would go into his growing business. That wasn't going to happen. It didn't happen.

Coming of age in a Jewish home with an Irish mother and an Eastern European Jewish father prepared him well for the Chelsea experience. Arnie came to Chelsea first with me in 1966, when he was sixteen and I was fifteen. We visited my father's drugstore. I walked him around Chelsea Square. I drove him up and down the city's streets. This was before the Chelsea Fire of 1973, the second major fire to destroy a large part of the dying city that had not yet been carted away and buried. My Marblehead friends felt uneasy in Chelsea. Not Arnie. Even then, we liked that not everything about life had to appear to be neatly in order. In 1967, Chelsea society straddled that broken place between the past and the present, and it stood there for many years. The established Chelsea population was large enough to provide continuity, while the arrival of several thousand non-English-speaking Puerto Ricans who lived in its most decrepit housing stock gave outsiders another chance to deride the place as a junk pile and an ugly dump. That's how our friends from Marblehead viewed Chelsea. "Some dump," Mr. Quigley would often say in response to such a view expressed about the city by those who did not understand its secrets and its strengths.

Shortly before Arnie came to Chelsea in 1977, he lived on a New Hampshire farm while attending graduate school, studying history and economics. He wanted to use photography as a tool to explore and analyze the history of economics, to learn about and to photograph images reflecting the real-time product of industrialism, wealth, wages, valuations, classes and inequality. Arnie found in Chelsea a profound visual reality—a train wreck—and an unrehearsed, unadorned picture of poverty. He found day-to-day reality stark and powerful for Chelsea's mostly lower-income and welfare-poor residents. Images of inequality and poverty became his obsession. The way people lived—this is what he wanted to capture. "I saw clarity and truth," he told me. "No one wanted to be reminded of this type of poverty and inequality. Powerful images were everywhere."

47

2

POLITICAL ECONOMY

Every two years, the mayoral election process energized the political scene in Chelsea. The city spun in perpetual motion like a political top during election years. (Before 1927, mayoral elections happened every year.) Many people wanted to be the mayor of Chelsea, and so they ran for election, or reelection, during the years of turmoil. Politics was always the salve—the distraction from the poverty and corruption that abounded all around, much of it in plain sight.

Political lines were always drawn in Chelsea. Everything that mattered was economic at its base and political in its philosophy. The political boundaries were drawn along ethnic lines between the Irish, the Jews, the Polish and the Italians, the inheritors of everything Chelsea—its poverty, its personality, its inescapability. People felt free to express their political views freely to neighbors and to friends and relatives. Chelsea people complained bitterly about the Red Sox and glorified the Celtics, the Patriots and the Bruins' Bobby Orr. Mayoral races, like sporting events, were a spectator sport. Those running city hall, whose relatives had run city hall for thirty years, and the longtime outsider factions who wanted in again clashed like football rivals in a crowded stadium.

Arnie and I covered about twelve election cycles—a combination of aldermanic races and mayoral contests—from the years 1977 to 1990. The future always beckoned during an election year in tired, beaten-down Chelsea. The two-square-mile city became a battlefield of sorts between competing constituencies.

Pledge of Allegiance at the opening of a city council meeting.

Ward 4 alderman Bobby Bishop.

The in-crowd, the old Chelsea characters and political personalities—those in control of the mayor's office—dearly wanted to hold on to power. They felt much safer when they opted for the tried-and-true instead of taking chances. New ideas were doomed in a political environment where popularity, above all, determined your value as a politician.

The city's political economy dragged it and its people lower and lower into a death-defying spiral. In Chelsea, public corruption, inertia and revenge politics became institutionalized during the twentieth century. This was the business model of governing the city. The mayors during the turbulent years—Joel Pressman, Tom Mace, Jimmy Mitchell, Tommy Nolan and Butch Brennen—dominated political life. They were the major voter draws in all the wards. In addition, a subset of board of aldermen and school committee members like Richard "Richie" Clayman, Mark Levine, Leo Robinson, Larry Sullivan, Ted "Teddy" Smigielski, Eddie O'Neill, Elizabeth McBride and Chubby Tiro are just some of the names that readily come to mind. Tom Birmingham, who never ran for municipal office in Chelsea, became the president of the state senate. He attended Harvard and Harvard Law School and became a Rhodes Scholar. "I remain more Chelsea than Cambridge," he noted in most of his speeches delivered locally. "This serves me well."

But Andrew Quigley had risen higher than all of them already, during the early 1950s. His family name and reputation dwarfed the others, but so did the negatives of living in such a small place and so toxic a political environment. The Quig, or the Senator, as Andrew Quigley was most often called, had served as mayor, state senator, state senator and mayor at the same time and state representative—all before he was twenty-five years old. "You know, Josh, I was senator, mayor and rep at a very young age, and if I hadn't screwed up my life, I might have been governor," he said to me inside his office one morning when I first began with him at the *Chelsea Record*. "And now look at what my life has come to. I'm sitting here talking with you!" His satire, his sardonic twist on everything, was a means of lamenting his life and what it had come to. It was also part of his enormous personality, his ability to act and tell the story of his life.

As the long-serving chairman of the Chelsea School Committee, Mr. Quigley ruled the public schools with an iron constitution and fist. Although he would rather have been the mayor, he became unelectable during the mid-1950s. He never caught fire again with the voters. The winning Quigley voter demographic shrank. He was relegated to serving on the school committee only and exclusively. He was elected and reelected every election

Left to right: The Senator, publisher Andrew Quigley; D.A. Newman Flanagan; Sheriff Dennis Kearney; and Mayor Tom Nolan, 1986.

during this period. His voice, the most eloquent at city hall, dominated all the others. He stood head and shoulders above them all. The smarter ones among them, like Joel Pressman, hated Mr. Quigley and feared him.

The chairman of the school committee and the publisher of the *Chelsea Record* was the most powerful man in city politics. He could give out more jobs than the mayor. He could hire, and he could fire. His editorial support in the newspaper's columns could make or break a candidacy. More often than not, they did. If you challenged him directly and appeared to mean it, he would chase you and dog you until you were defeated.

When he was running for reelection to the school committee in 1978, I asked him during a morning visit to his office: "Is there anything I can do for you, Mr. Quigley?" My publisher and boss looked at me, smiled and replied, "Yes, Josh. You want to help me get reelected? Why don't you drive back to Marblehead to your father's house, run upstairs to your bedroom and lock yourself inside your room until the election is over. Do this and you will be helping me more than you can imagine." I came to admire and love Mr. Quigley overnight because he was so smart, so much fun, so quick with his wit and possessed by such an amazingly honest and comedic sense of humor. "Remember, Josh," he liked to say to me, "The

U.S. senator from Massachusetts Paul Tsongas (1941–1997) with Andrew Quigley, visiting the *Chelsea Record*'s Broadway office, 1981.

truth is a terrible weapon of aggression. The last thing anyone wants to hear about themselves is the truth."

Mr. Quigley once ran for Congress at the height of his power, or his madness, however one chooses to look at being a political prodigy in Chelsea. He lost that election to the incumbent, Thomas Lane. During one of our daily morning meetings inside his office at the *Chelsea Record*, I asked him why he lost. "I lost because I went against what my father tried to teach me," he said, matter-of-fact. "He warned me about Congressman Lane. I told him I could beat him and that nothing was going to stop me. Yet he warned me again and again. Don't run against him." "Why didn't he want you to run against him?" I asked. "Never run against a congressman who's in jail," his father warned him, he told me. Lane had run his reelection campaign from jail and beat Mr. Quigley. "I should have listened to my father," he repeated. Quigley looked inward all the time and had a stunning propensity for powerful self-deprecation.

We learned early on from Andrew Quigley that politics in Chelsea was something of its own making, practiced with a fervor and an intensity all its own. Mr. Quigley lived for politics. No one in the city understood elections and promises made better than him. The *Chelsea Record* welcomed the elections. The political advertising helped to keep the paper afloat during this era when everything about the city had changed.

"Awakening is a political activity in Chelsea," Mr. Quigley told us when we first arrived. We had no idea what he meant exactly, but we would soon find out. Awakening in Chelsea connoted the act of preparing oneself to enter the fray as political subjects, every day, again and again, ad infinitum, ad nauseum. Mr. Quigley understood, as Sigmund Freud tells us, that awakening in the morning and looking at oneself in the mirror is all about the act of constituting identity. Preparing oneself for a walk to the corner store at the beginning of a new day was also a political activity. Politics in Chelsea was never about education or status but all about identity (what we today call "identity politics") and always about economics.

Mr. Quigley had a way of explaining politics that turned long-established beliefs upside down. Early one morning I broke a story in Mr. Quigley's office at the *Chelsea Record* on Fourth Street. A well-known, popular person had declared his candidacy for mayor. Standing by Mr. Quigley's desk, reading from my reporter's notebook, I told him that Bud McCormick (not the real name of the candidate) announced he was running for mayor of Chelsea. "He's an appliance salesman, a wife beater and an alcoholic," I said to Mr. Quigley. "He didn't even graduate from high school," I added. Mr. Quigley looked up at me. "Appliance salesman, wife beater and alcoholic who didn't graduate from high school," he repeated. "Thoroughly qualified to be the mayor of Chelsea, Josh." Mr. Quigley had a wide array of people visit his office every day: a six-hundred-pound man named "Tiny"; a boxer with a flattened nose named "Champ" who never won a fight; "Donuts" Robinson; "Pickles" Nyman's partner in a Chelsea Square laundry business; and on and on. He was his father's son, never underestimating the common man or throwing him under the bus.

Early on in our relationship, I came to Mr. Quigley wanting to do an investigative report on a corrupt Chelsea police captain. He dismissed the idea with a mix of contempt and mock indignation. "Josh, if you want to do an investigation why don't you start by investigating yourself!" he said to me. He made his points with comments like that. I was always amazed by his sarcasm, his use of irony and his general disrespect for uninformed opinions made by people who couldn't run a corner store, let alone manage a city like Chelsea. Tolstoy referred to those types as the ignorant masses—but Mr. Quigley would dare not describe voters in the city he loved that way.

Mr. Quigley did not allow investigative reporting to appear in the *Chelsea Record*. He read investigative reporting in the *Boston Globe*. Investigative reporting caused him to feel uneasy. The city was too small, with too many of its key players connected by blood and political allegiances to publish the real truth about the Chelsea people who ran the place without hurting the newspaper. Mr. Quigley feared the truth as much as he professed to like it.

As Chelsea edged closer and closer to social, economic and political ruin, preservation of the old, the vain and the stupid was pro forma for mayoral success. What was known had greater validity and promise than what was portrayed as new. Those on the outside of the ruling order at city hall wanted in. Their chance-taking was of a different kind. Beyond city hall's epic ineptitude and indifference, voters abhorred its disregard for honesty. The threat of city hall's retribution against those yearning for a change in the political order, or those demanding to be heard, silenced many before they spoke.

Mr. Quigley often joked about Chelsea's economic difficulties, its history of fires and the changing times the city seemed inured to. "We don't worry about recessions here," he said to me in 1977. "Oh really, why is that?" I asked. "Because we've been in a depression for fifty years!" This was as much political banter as it was economic reality.

Though many residents believed it was dying, Chelsea remained viable in 1977. It was kept alive by its incredible mixture of people from all walks of life who tended to get along, for better or worse. It was a place where racism was not a part of the fabric of the place (except for the Puerto Ricans excluded from public life, which was more about politics than racism), but ethnic loyalties were paramount where violent crime was low and race riots were nonexistent. Everyone was someone in this era of Chelsea's political economy. Those who loved the place felt they had nowhere to move. For a great deal of the impoverished population, going elsewhere was not an option. "Besides, where could we go and where could we live but here?" was the popular refrain.

The local economy sputtered, however, and the population decline continued. Whatever was bad got worse. Chelsea was a wide-open place for gambling, for drugs, for booze. One could hide out in Chelsea because no one from the outside wanted to come here, though nearly every major Democratic politician from Massachusetts visited this stronghold.

Another peculiarity about the Chelsea experience was talking with those who had abandoned the city for the suburbs, who professed loving Chelsea and everything about their lives when they were there but who would not consider living in the city because it wasn't good enough for their children. You could live your life without leaving. Many did just that.

Polaski Day, Chelsea Square.

Bongo drummers, Bosson Playground, Ward 1, 1983.

Salvation Army at war, Broadway 1979.

Above: Fledgling U.S. congressman Ed Markey with supporters, 1978.

Left: Joe Kennedy, CEO of Citizen Energy (*right*), and Governor Michael Dukakis touring Metropolitan Energy, Lower Broadway, 1979.

From 1977 to 1990, the outflow of old families accelerated. New families weren't moving into Chelsea, except for the Puerto Ricans, who were moving in everywhere across the city, into all of its wards. Most Puerto Ricans did not speak English, did not register to vote and therefore did not vote. Most were poverty-stricken, uneducated apartment dwellers in the worst housing in the moribund wards of the city. It took Puerto Ricans a long period of residency in Chelsea to understand that they didn't exist to the city's politicians and elected officials, that they added nothing of any economic consequence to sway the vote, unless and until they began voting in larger numbers.

Puerto Ricans mostly settled in Ward 2, the once crowded, entirely Jewish neighborhood of the city south of the commercial corridor of Everett Avenue that had spread eastward to the end of Broadway, where it ends at the Mystic River under the Tobin Bridge. Though battered and crumbling—largely empty after the second Great Chelsea Fire in 1973, which swept away the bulk of it—Ward 2 was the epicenter of Chelsea politics for more than half a century. Historically, it was largely the residence of the city's Jews and Polish, Democrats all, engaged and hustling members of the community trying to rise up and out in a rush to improve themselves and move to the suburbs. The heartbeat of political Chelsea measured itself by political activity in this ward.

Neighbors gathering, Ward 2.

Map of Chelsea's wards, 1960.

As the 1977 mayoral election unfolded, Ward 2 was dead on arrival. Many of its streets were lined with empty three-deckers built after the disastrous 1908 fire. Marginal small businesses that had seen better days—the delis, varieties, barbershops, tailors, real estate offices and corner drugstores of my father's generation—remained, but the vast majority of them had disappeared, leaving empty storefronts. All the glitter of this turn-of-the-century wonderland (which resembled the *Godfather Part II*'s re-creation of the bustling Lower East Side) was irretrievably gone in 1977 at the dawn of our careers as journalists at the *Chelsea Record*.

The majority of the Chelsea vote from its remaining Anglo Saxon residents—who could be counted on to come out on Election Day—resided in Ward 4, a neighborhood to the northwest spanning the length of Washington Avenue to Revere Beach Parkway, to the top of Powderhorn Hill, where the Soldier's Home remains today.

Ward 5, defined by the Prattville and Woodlawn neighborhoods, maintained itself as the last bastion of the white middle class and provided the second-largest voting bloc. Removed from the chaos and the negative

View from Powderhorn Hill, Ward 4.

energy afflicting all the wards on the other side of Revere Beach Parkway, Prattville's orderly and clean persona prevailed. The same is true today.

Nevertheless, this coming 1977 election, and all subsequent elections we covered, were battles forming out of the old meeting the new, the young competing with the old, for the only prize that seems to have mattered—the mastery of Chelsea City Hall and the jobs and influence available there.

The old tried-and-true demographic—that is, those who registered and those who voted—would pick the next mayor every two years. This demographic consisted of older residents in their sixties and up, the first-generation descendants of immigrants who had come to America from Europe at the turn of the twentieth century. They looked like relics from another age walking the gritty streets of the collapsing city. Older folks, poverty-stricken, dressed poorly. Limping. On crutches. Carrying canes. Overweight. Ill. The veritable walking wounded of American society. They were the majority of Chelsea's voting public.

The place was in a state of unstoppable decline, still vibrant to those who could appreciate it but the equivalent of a patient on oxygen in intensive care. The streets were in disrepair and dirty, filled with trash and the bric-a-brac of the struggle to survive. The whole place needed a good coat of paint for its many wooden structures and a solid mortar

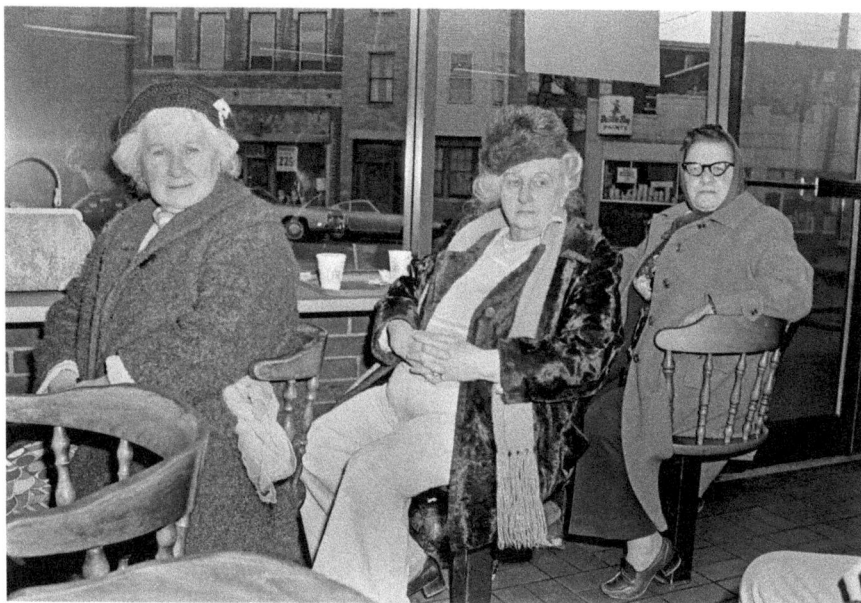

Longtime Chelsea residents and patrons of Riley's Roast Beef.

pointing for all its brick buildings. Absentee landlords owned much of the property, a mix of the industrial and the residential, one indiscernible from the other, as the two communities lived literally next door and atop of one another. The city was then, and remains today, a hodgepodge of industry and commerce living in a hopelessly polluted environment (the subject of the last chapter in this volume).

The business community—what remained of it—led by American Biltrite, Cabot Paints and Stain, the Sweetheart Paper Company and Kayem Foods paid little heed to the meanderings of local politics. Business owners tried to stay as far away from the contests at city hall as possible. They were the city's largest employers along with the multinational petroleum corporations Mobile and Exxon, whose presence dominated the industrial Chelsea waterfront. Still, the private enterprises and the dreaded public sector rarely intersected in Chelsea.

Kids in Chelsea were inventive about how they kept themselves occupied. They played pickup street hockey under the expressway or skipped rope in Quigley Park, rode their bikes all over, went fishing in the polluted Chelsea Creek or played stickball on the streets wherever they lived. Everything was about improvisation for kids growing up in Chelsea. The city's parks and public places were in disrepair. Swings didn't last a week. Basketball

Longtime Chelsea residents.

Left: Kayem Foods factory workers making hot dogs.

Below: Jumping rope in Quigley Park.

Street hockey under the Expressway, near the Williams School.

netting didn't have a chance. Kids wrecked, broke and destroyed whatever they could.

Public housing was a sorry mess of rundown, substandard living spaces wholly unfit for habitation but better than nothing to those who occupied them. The Housing Authority was broke. Waitlists got doctored. Some waited forever without receiving a subsidized apartment. Others got theirs instantly because of who they knew. Liquor stores were located everywhere throughout the city's wards. In many of the city's squares, liquor stores lined both sides of the street.

The Department of Public Works vehicles were bent and rusted. The bright-orange city trash trucks plied streets with sidewalks piled high with mattresses and broken furniture, with the garbage and odd trash spilling onto the city's streets from corner to corner on pickup days. On hot summer days, the place stank of the garbage hurled into the trucks, bits and pieces of it scattered everywhere by toughened city workers working savagely to get the pickups finished.

The public schools could barely fund themselves. They were unfit to meet or manage the challenges of the changing times and the great wave of Spanish-speaking immigrants now populating them. There was not a single Spanish-speaking police officer, firefighter, city employee or teacher

Lower Broadway Bandits, Ward 2.

Broadway Bikers.

inside all of these institutions as the mayoral campaign got underway in 1977. The only police officer who supposedly spoke Spanish (but was barely able to string together two or three sentences) was an older, red-headed, pink-skinned Irish police captain named Al Sweeney. He had taken a course to learn Spanish in an effort to show how the Chelsea Police Department was changing with the times. The situation hadn't changed very much when the city went into receivership in 1992.

Puerto Ricans from smaller towns like Cabo Rojo on the south coast of the island immigrated to Chelsea to can vegetables at the Suffolk Farms factory on Park Street. Severe poverty on the island of Puerto Rico drove the first residents to settle in Chelsea in the late 1950s and many thousands more by the mid-1960s. The Mercados and the Toros were among the oldest of those Puerto Rican families. They lived in my family's building in Chelsea Square for many years. When I was growing up and working behind the counter in my father's drugstore, Jose Toro and Jimmy Mercado worked as clerks with me. Their poverty when they arrived, and for many years to follow, was severe.

Many property owners refused to rent to darker-skinned Spanish speakers. But others in need of tenants for their dilapidated properties in the Chelsea of this bleak economic period rented to the Puerto Ricans. Landlords were

Chestnut Street fire aftermath with Officer Sullivan.

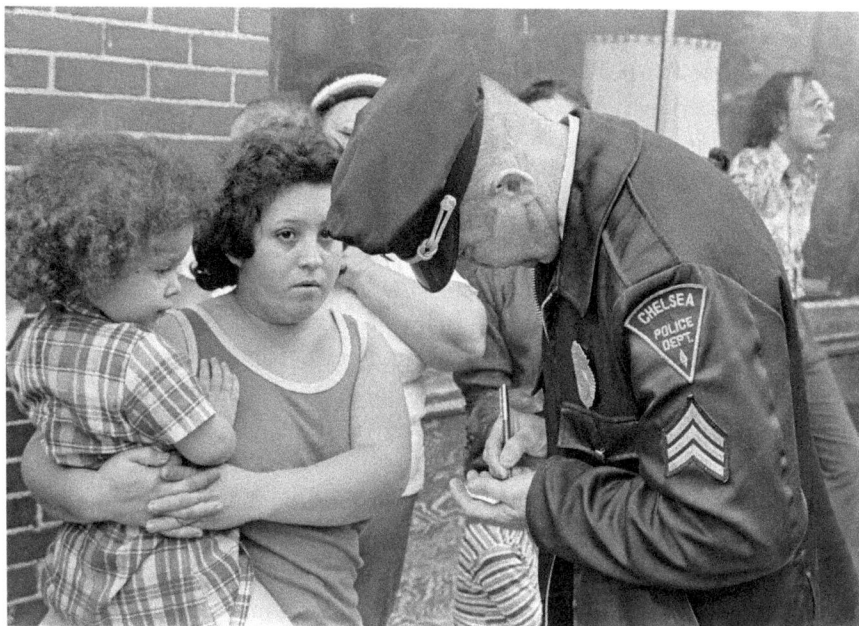

Fire victim giving a statement to the police.

happy to get their rent for substandard, worn-down, cold-water flat housing with a gas-on-gas stove for heat in the kitchen.

On some streets, Puerto Ricans moved in and the remaining white population said goodbye and moved out. The city's public face changed dramatically. New Chelsea residents replaced Jewish and Irish families that had dominated the daily life of the city for several generations. Formerly Jewish and Irish neighborhoods became unrecognizable—not so much because of the Puerto Ricans but in addition to their presence in places where they were never seen before. St. Rose Church, the parish church for the Chelsea Irish, became the Puerto Rican church.

The division between whites and Puerto Ricans was noticeable, especially at the police station, where Puerto Ricans were now being arrested for drug possession and carrying knives, for disturbing the peace and theft in numbers disproportionate to their population during this period long before police profiling became recognizable. The old-line white gangsters, number writers, bookmakers and sellers of stolen merchandise all flourished in front of the eyes of the white police. City officials looked the other way for Anglo landlords and property owners whose buildings failed codes. It was into those buildings that Puerto Rican families came to bring up their children.

Puerto Ricans remained separate from Anglo Chelsea. Every effort was made at every level in Chelsea society to exclude Puerto Ricans in one way or another or to deride their presence as the coming of the end. The prevailing thought shared openly among much of the captive Anglo population was that the Puerto Ricans needed to understand how being free in America really works, and especially how being free works in Chelsea.

Chelsea City Hall would teach them everything they needed to know—that is, everything about second-class treatment—as a race of people, let alone as new citizens of the city. It bears repeating that Anglo Chelsea did not welcome men and women from Puerto Rico. During this early period in their residency, Puerto Ricans were reviled, misunderstood and as unwelcome as the first white settlers were to the Sagamore Indians living here when Chelsea was founded in 1624.

The police went after Puerto Ricans disproportionately in cracking down on the rampant drug trade. The drug trade and violence, brutality and indifference weren't the domain only of Puerto Ricans and other Hispanics. Heroin, the primary choice of the Hispanic community (but not entirely), was plentiful and cheap. Nearly everyone else in the drug trade got away scot-free. The angry poor white criminal element also kept the police busy. The police were paid to look the other way for the white gangsters running the city's organized crime elements.

Almost all of the city's meaningful institutions were failing by comparison to what came before. The chamber of commerce, the Rotary and the Kiwanis Clubs, the parent-teacher organizations, the Polish, Irish and French Clubs, everything was going in the wrong direction. Holiday celebrations, parades and memorial services for the veterans from Chelsea who served in the World Wars, Korea and Vietnam had largely begun a disappearing act.

These clubs, once the center of the city's historic connection to its immigrant past, had become drinking clubs and political forums. At the French Club in Mill Hill, for example, no French members remained. Arnie and I covered the well-attended, even boisterous, political rallies held at the Irish Club in Mill Hill, the French Club on Spencer Avenue and the Polish Political Club (PPC) on Lower Broadway. Only the PPC remains today as a rental event venue.

Fiery speeches, drunken crowds, adoring supporters and spies all mingled together at these clubs in the days and weeks before a mayoral election. The speeches on both sides were all the same; everyone's performance was hideous. Banality was always rewarded with applause. The raucous political

Broadway Parade.

Kids planting flags on veterans' graves, Memorial Day, Garden Cemetery.

times at private clubs, where speeches were made and thousands of dollars raised, are now part of a vanished past.

A barroom society flourished in Chelsea. About thirty barrooms and another ten private drinking clubs dotted the city. With names like Jimmy's, the Chelsea Walk Pub, Ryan's, the Merit Club and the Cary Square Club, places for drinking and drugging became a commonplace part of existence for your average longtime Chelsea resident.

Inside those barrooms and private clubs, illegal betting generated tens of thousands of dollars a week on sporting events, poker machines and video games on steroids. The bar owners and the game machine owners got rich, and the police who allowed the illegal machines to flourish got paid a great deal more than their salaries revealed. At the Beacon Café, which Arnie and I owned from 1982 to 1991, video gaming machines were not allowed. This caused the Beacon to be visited by a corrupt police captain on the take. This is how distorted the enforcement of the law had become—those not using illegal gaming machines were punished while those who had them were protected from punishment.

Inside the Harmony Bar, on Fifth Street, the epicenter of illegal gaming and video machine ownership (and most of Chelsea's illegal infrastructure), the city's "King of Crime" Sammy Berkowitz was present

Chelsea's "King of Crime," Sammy Berkowitz (*left*), with Broadway National Bank owner and president Jack Tierney, 1983.

every day, playing one-hundred-dollar games of gin rummy, smoking Pall Malls and sipping Great Western Champagne from miniature bottles. Nearly every day, Berkowitz trekked to the Broadway National Bank in Bellingham Square with a large brown paper shopping bag of cash in tow. Cops picked up their smaller bags of money every Friday at the Harmony. Even FBI agent H. Paul Rico visited Berkowitz at the Harmony on Fridays for his gratuity. The pedestrian mobs crowding Bellingham Square exulted at Berkowitz's daily appearances.

Here was a real-time Chelsea legend. A cab driver who turned gambling entrepreneur when he hit the number for $50,000 on any given betting game, Berkowitz was worth in the tens of millions of dollars during this era. Five feet, ten inches tall, about 180 pounds, balding, poorly dressed, with oversized capped white teeth and inarticulate, he paraded around in public for everyone to see him. In a way, he was the mayor of Fifth Street, the city's center of crime.

In 1980, Berkowitz received a presidential pardon from Ronald Reagan. He carried it with him in the inside pocket of the long coat he wore during the winter months. "Sammy. Sammy. Show us your presidential pardon," the crowds would urge the King of Crime. He'd pull the document from his inside pocket and display it proudly. "How'd you get it Sammy? How'd you get it?" he was often asked. He'd pull the Pall Mall from his lips. "Like everything else I get. I bought it!" When you wonder how patently open and public crime can exist in a city, the Chelsea model holds true. Officials were paid off. Crime flourished.

The entire apparatus of municipal government operated fraudulently or at least with the taint of fraud. If corruption had been removed from the government, the government would have ceased to exist. The mayor's $20,000 annual salary contributed to the problem—so much so that the poverty-level salary, among those who understood how government works, bore no relationship whatsoever to what the mayor got paid. "How can anyone afford to be the mayor of Chelsea?" I asked Mr. Quigley inside the newsroom at the *Chelsea Record*. "What do you mean, Josh?" he asked in return. "How can the mayor survive on $20,000 a year?" "The W-2 doesn't tell the whole story about the mayor's salary," he replied.

Dramatic, steep, unrelenting economic, political and social decline marked this period. In 1960, seventeen corner drugstores existed. By 1977, there were four left. Several dozen doctors served the city's population for decades. By the time Arnie and I got there, only a handful remained. A dozen tailors and seamstresses made careers taking care of Chelsea residents' garments.

Above: Hy's Shoes, Broadway, 1980. The store closed after a fire destroyed it. Owner, alderman and Mayor-elect Mark Levine was accused of and tried for arson but never convicted.

Left: Syd Selesnick in front of his haberdashery, Syd's.

Nearly all of them disappeared. A half-dozen delicatessens—open all hours of the day and night—provided Chelsea its food heartbeat. They all closed their doors. Even the Chelsea Memorial Hospital closed in 1979.

Broadway businesses like Hy's Shoes, men's haberdasheries Syd's, Nat Weiner's and Robert Hall and Gorin's department store all closed their doors before 1980. Broadway's five-and-dime—JJ Newbury's—didn't make it to 1980.

In 1960, thirteen synagogues opened their doors every day for the old Jews who filed inside for morning services. By 1977, there were six. By 1987, there were three. The largest and most glorious, still active, is Congregation Agudath Shalom, otherwise known as the Walnut Street Synagogue. My grandfather Louis Resnek was an original founder of the Walnut Street Synagogue in 1910. Some of the closed synagogues on Chestnut and Shurtleff Streets became Iglesias de Dios—Churches of God—for the Spanish-speaking.

Iglesias de Dios Spanish-speaking Catholic church at the site of a former synagogue on Chestnut Street.

73

Inside the orthodox Walnut Street synagogue, looking down from the women's balcony.

Churches became shells of what they used to be. St. Rose Church, long the center of Catholic life in Chelsea, had a largely Spanish-speaking membership. As the number of these congregants rose, Irish members moved down to the French church on Broadway. Founded in the 1820s, the Baptist church on Shurtleff Street, with its rich but grainy orange-hued Cape Ann granite exterior, attracted a large crowd of businessmen once a year seeking out a traditional fin and haddie dinner served up by the remaining white-haired older women members. By 1987, its membership was all but extinct.

By 1987, Chelsea's transition had moved up a few clicks with the arrival of newcomers, urban pioneers, younger people pushed out of Boston by rising housing prices and everything else, discovering Chelsea and loving it because rents were lower. The place, they believed, had a certain charm. After all, at two miles from downtown Boston, Chelsea was so close it was like living in Boston. The French might say Chelsea had panache to the outsiders coming in. But as Mr. Quigley said over and over, "We look out our windows at Boston for half the price that Boston residents look out through their windows at us." The city had a panache of sorts: a bad image but a good heart, a sorry economy but a vibrant people.

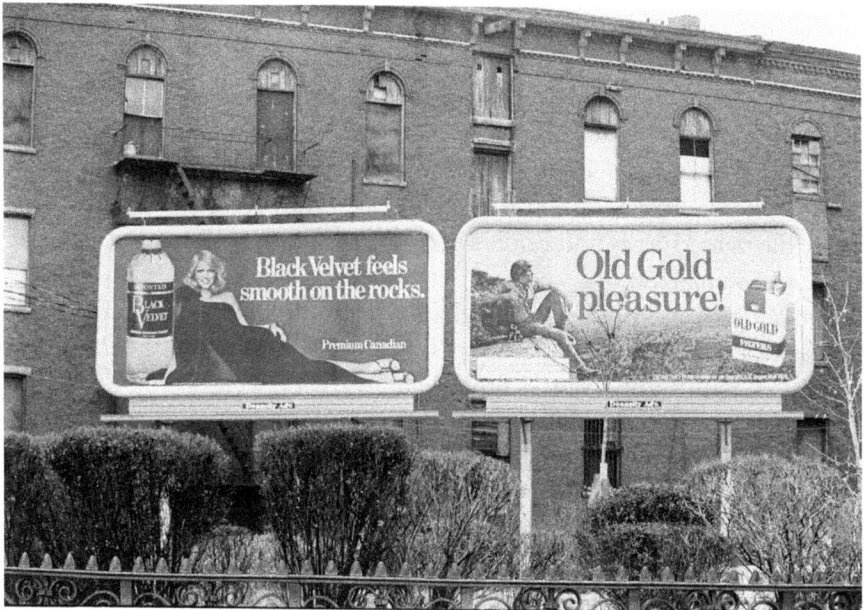

Billboards, Chelsea Square

Food was always a common denominator, not just for feeding oneself, but for hanging out in Chelsea society from morning to morning, day to day, week to week, year to year. The city's delis offered up great food at all hours of the day and night. Two of them, Pressman's on Central Avenue and Murray and Eddie's on Broadway, served corned beef, barrel pickles and potato salad such as could not be found in all the surrounding cities. During our time in Chelsea, Pressman's and Murray and Eddie's were to die for. Mrs. Pressman's cabbage soup served with black bread and butter and a plate of pickles was a culinary delight.

At Pressman's Deli, owner Sam Pressman, in his late eighties, was as ornery as they came in Chelsea. He presided with a cigar implanted in his mouth, generally insulting most of his customers, especially those who had moved out of Chelsea but who returned for their corned beef. "Sam, I want my corned beef very lean," said an older wealthy former Chelsea Jewish woman dressed in her finery standing at the counter inside his Central Avenue deli. "Where do you live now?" Pressman asked her. "Newton," she said, her flashy diamond ring and fur coat a stark contrast to the run-down deli. "You want your corned beef lean?" Pressman answered, taking his cigar out of his mouth. "Then go back to Newton and get it lean!"

The menu inside Murray and Eddie's deli on Broadway highlighted sandwiches named after gregarious, successful and well-liked local lawyers like the Al Levinson, a tongue sandwich with mustard and sour kraut; the Richie Clayman, a corned beef sandwich with Swiss cheese on dark rye; and the Evan Gellar, a pastrami sandwich with sliced pickles and potato salad. Three brothers—Sam, Eddie and Murray—ran the place for thirty years. When it closed, they were left with nothing to show for their lifetime spent inside the deli. Murray and Eddie's disappeared one day like everything else in the vanishing city.

Sub shops like Storti's in Bellingham Square, smaller supermarkets like Goldstein's in Cary Square, Promisel's next to the post office (the Promisels lived next door to the Resneks on Williams Street during the height of the immigrant era) and the Blackstone on Broadway made travel to shopping centers or larger supermarkets, now the norm, seem like trips into the impersonal world the average Chelsea resident wanted no part of.

Rita's Sub Shop, which morphed into Rita's Fine Italian Restaurant on Winissimett Street and then into Rita's Catering in Everett, is today the second-largest catering group in Massachusetts. In Chelsea, Rita's found a great and admiring audience. For the first time, Chelsea had a destination restaurant that served fine food. Rita Rossi ruled. By 1990, she was gone.

Sam Pressman, counter of Pressman's Deli.

Murray (*left*), Eddy (*center*) and Sam Rosenberg inside their deli Murray & Eddy's on the day it closed.

The Chelsea YMHA (Young Men's Hebrew Association) drew a mixed crowd, mostly non-Jewish, to its gym, located on the second floor of a former synagogue on Clark Avenue. The synagogue was built in 1938 and shut its doors in the 1950s before reopening as the YMHA. You could play basketball in the competitive Wild Animal League on a court where the sacred Torah used to be stored inside the tabernacle of the main sanctuary. The rabbi's private study became the steam room. You could then sun yourself on the deck at the back of the building after having a steam. Lawyers, doctors, business owners, athletes and nonathletes grew up here back when young men coming up—angry men, whites and blacks, young and old, a sprinkling of Jews, Hispanics and whatever—all mixed together at the YMHA every day, Club Chelsea's central control at its enduring best.

When we came to the city in 1977, Chock Glazer ran the place and was its heart and soul. Glazer was a popular former great Chelsea High School athlete from the late 1950s who had a longing to bring everyone together through sports and competition at the YMHA. The place closed in 1986. "Not enough Jewish members," said the folks at the Combined Jewish Philanthropies. Through Glazer and because of him, a former synagogue cum Chelsea meeting place brought together a dozen races and religions until it closed.

The Thanksgiving Day high school football game at Chelsea Memorial Stadium brought out a huge crowd from year to year. The rivalry between Chelsea and adjacent Everett High Schools made Chelsea appear to be a normal American community in the public light. Cheerleaders, proudly wearing their red-and-black Chelsea Devils uniforms, shouted out their rhymes. Young men played their hearts out on the football field and became athletic heroes whose exploits were later reported on the sports pages of the *Chelsea Record*. Thanksgiving dinners followed in their apartments and homes. The rivalry with neighboring Everett, dating back to the 1890s, ended in 1986.

On the Fourth of July at Memorial Stadium, fireworks lit up the sky and always attracted huge crowds. In what some suburbanites might consider a dystopian celebration, kids with sparklers ran around wildly screaming amid midget wrestlers, carnival rides and games of chance. Adults drank, and younger people smoked joints in public. This in-your-face entertainment suited Chelsea and was tolerated by the police. If you didn't like Chelsea, too bad. Then don't come here. You think you're better than Chelsea because you live elsewhere, good luck to you seemed the mantra. Pretense and affect had no place in the society of this era.

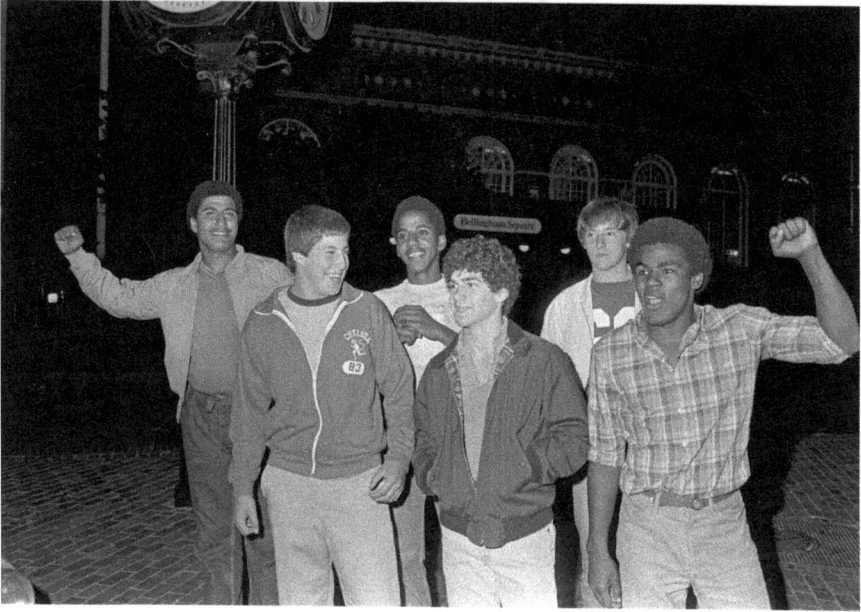

Out at night in the square.

The majority of the population existed in true lower-middle and working-class fashion—living from week-to-week, paycheck-to-paycheck, working locally and owning small-scale mom-and-pop retail shops. The welfare class simmered and lingered, trapped in their economic conundrum in a place where they found plenty of company. A few very rich and well-to-do families persisted, but there was not much of an upper middle class to speak of. Existence in Chelsea rested on tradition, heritage and a fierce, almost blind pride in coming from this place.

Chelsea people shared oneness—the common bond, coming from this place called Chelsea—so small and so hidden away from the mainstream that it shouldn't have existed. Politics glued everyone and everything relevant about the place together. The one connection shared by nearly all was their relationship to Chelsea City Hall. Who you were was not a manifestation of your wealth or the lack of it, your education or your poverty. Rather, who you were, what you were all about, was how you interacted inside the small city, who you could ask a favor of, who your friends were at city hall.

City hall could order your street cleaned. It could get you public housing. City hall could have the police patrol your neighborhood. City hall could give your kid a summer job working the parks—and city hall could remake

Ladies in Bellingham Square.

Sign of the times, Chelsea Square.

the parks from time to time. City hall could ruin your life if you were an absentee landlord. The building department might send its inspectors to your decrepit property and close it down or force you to fix it up. The absentee landlords who had moved to Brookline and Newton, Marblehead and Swampscott lost their insider status. If you were a Chelsea insider and the owner of slum properties, city hall didn't bother with you. City hall could lower your taxes if you knew one of the assessors (chiefly David Newman, who ran that office). If your kid got in trouble and was hauled into the Chelsea Courthouse in Chelsea Square, David Greenspan, the chief probation officer, would take care of that. Everyone got a second and third chance with Greenspan.

"The two Davids," as they were known—David Newman and David Greenspan—both short Jewish gentlemen and Chelsea natives who came of age during the late 1930s and 1940s, ran the city outside of city hall from Newman's butcher shop on Addison Street and Greenspan's office inside the Victorian courthouse. They exerted their power over the city for three decades and remained in the highest esteem of those they helped out until the day they died.

City assessor David Newman (*left*) and Alderman Richie Clayman, 1980.

Joshua A. Resnek

JOSHUA RESNEK says that he will stand-up to Aldermen who make a mockery of what an alderman ought to be.

He says he will stand-up to Aldermen who have lost faith in this city's future and who belittle and humiliate developers, public officials and even their colleagues in the weak effort to advance their own short-sighted desires.

It doesn't make any sense to return to office men who incessantly harp upon the obvious problems we commonly share.

Joshua Resnek believes that Chelsea has a great future. He believes that a young man, a college graduate, a property owner, a taxpayer, a writer in the city where his family has a long history, has a chance to be your Alderman at Large.

It doesn't make any sense to return to office the men who have lost their faith in Chelsea.

Vote for
JOSHUA A. RESNEK
Alderman - at - Large

Left: Joshua A. Resnek, alderman-at-large, *Chelsea Record* ad.

Below: Ward 2 alderman Ted Smigielski running for reelection, 1982.

During this turbulent era, there was no rhyme or reason for what got accomplished or what remained undone, what was destroyed or what remained intact. Municipal government responded to requests for funding from ward politicians. Ward politics attracted a garden variety of Chelsea residents, mostly common types of people, mostly men, who for some inexplicable combination of reasons, were popular among the residents of their wards. Usually, they came from older families with deeper roots in the city.

Politics dominated the Chelsea mainstream. It wasn't just who you were in Chelsea. It was about who you were supporting for mayor. During this era, politics soured. The pillars underpinning the political process produced winning politicians by emphasizing personal popularity over qualifications and sending them to city hall.

Mayoral elections in Chelsea were looked forward to like the coming of Christmas and with the importance of a significant religious or economic event. The mayor's two-year term guaranteed perpetual campaigning and political turmoil among the various candidates seeking the office. It also guaranteed political advertising in the *Chelsea Record*.

During a mayoral election year, the city was awash with street signs and automobiles with bumper stickers and campaign posters adorning many of

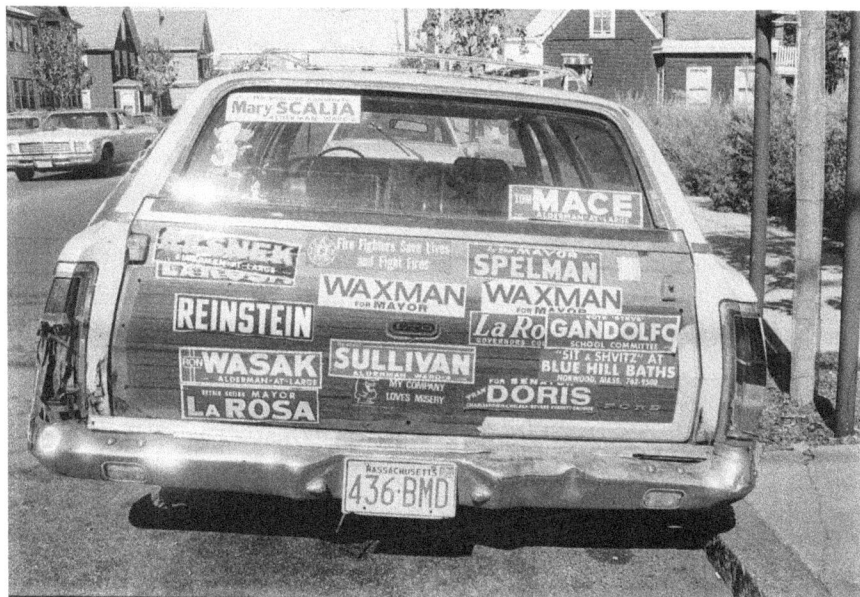

Station wagon covered with political stickers, early 1980s.

83

the city's small retail establishments up and down Broadway and throughout the city. Signs stood everywhere on wooden poles stuck into the ground in front of homes and apartment houses or raised higher on poles so they couldn't be torn down. With large hand-painted signs covering the windows, corner stores in the unlikeliest of buildings served as headquarters for both mayoral candidates.

The veneer of honesty expressed by the candidates hid the true nature of the cause: keeping the city hall gravy train on its track. Everything was geared toward guaranteeing the future flow of bribes and kickbacks. C-notes delivered folded up in surreptitious handshakes. Politicians awaiting such handshakes for "favors" done. Gangsters and illegal gaming bar-owners depositing thousands of dollars in cash nearly every day at the same bank teller's window. Inane boasts of power promising rewards accompanied by cheers of allegiance and blind loyalty. This was the eternal quid pro quo of the political economy, Chelsea style. The whole thing felt like one big, indecent joke.

Mr. Quigley viewed the election process like a professor of political science. He understood that none of what went on was an accident. It was all tried and true, set in cement throughout the decades, impervious to earthquakes. Elections were always the same. The winners and losers changed places from time to time.

Everyone loved being around their candidate. It was always exciting for Arnie and me to watch these election events play out, then return to the *Chelsea Record* to debrief Mr. Quigley. We'd then write up the story and develop the photographs. We laid out the paper. Mr. Quigley and his two sons, Stephen and Andrew, then worked on the press—catching the newspapers as they rolled off—tossed the papers into vans and station wagons and then delivered them throughout the city and to awaiting mobs in Bellingham Square the following day. On some days before an election, one thousand *Chelsea Records* could be sold in Bellingham Square by Al Goldman, whose hands were as black as printer's ink.

There were no such things in Chelsea as undecided voters or polling to measure a politician's strength or weakness. Polling couldn't work because Chelsea voters didn't answer honestly about who they were going to cast a ballot for. Besides, there was no middle choice.

Mr. Quigley understood the *Chelsea Record* was his platform to spread his beliefs and philosophy—and to sway the vote. If he didn't approve of the story I filed, if it did not fit his sense of amusement or his understanding of local political history, he'd toss it on the floor of the newsroom. Then he'd

Pressman for Mayor headquarters, 1977.

Reading the *Record* in Bellingham Square by city hall.

jump on it, twisting and crushing the piece with the soles of his sneakers. "This shit isn't going in my newspaper," he'd yell out. "Why not?" I'd reply. "Because the man who owns the press gets to print whatever he wants, that's why."

The *Chelsea Record* was popular with those who understood the human predicament and with fools who believed what they read. Mr. Quigley was not an aristocrat sailing down the Chelsea Creek on the presidential yacht. He was a Chelsea man who did not believe in aristocracy. He was without guilt, and as he often liked to say, "The worst thing about dishonest people is what they think of as honesty."

He liked fireworks. He excelled at civil war. Ineptitude upset him, but he always expected it to succeed over a new idea or the real thing. He was always ready to be disappointed by some of his allies and friends, and when they failed him, he tended to keep them around—since "the enemy of my enemy is my friend."

Election Day was the same, always. Chelsea was not alone in how its politics came of age during the various eras of dramatic economic and political change. What was unique to Chelsea was the size of the place—1.8 square miles, twenty-eight thousand residents—with its own police and fire departments, city traditions and long history. In reality, it should have been a ward of the city of Boston, except Boston had no use for Chelsea; it was too poor a place.

On Election Day during every mayoral race, sign-holders from opposing candidates stood like sentries in front of all the city's polling places: In front of St. Luke's Church in Ward 4, at the Chelsea Public Library across from city hall, in Chelsea Square at the Falcon's Nest Club, at the Polish Club just off Broadway downtown on Fourth Street (before it moved to lower Broadway), in the American Legion Hall across from the YMCA on Shurtleff Street and in front of the firehouse in Prattville. In a fictional Ward 6, that is, in Swampscott and Marblehead, where so many former Chelsea residents had moved, transplanted Chelseans awaited news of the results.

The grandstanding at city hall during council meetings, when the mayor clashed with whoever his opponent was, made even-handed reporting difficult and frustrating. These confrontations between candidates were publicity efforts aimed at using the *Chelsea Record* to get their message across. While the newspaper business, even the *Record*, was about the newspaper's right to exist and about its First Amendment right to express itself editorially, it was really more about a fourth dimension, giving municipal leaders running for

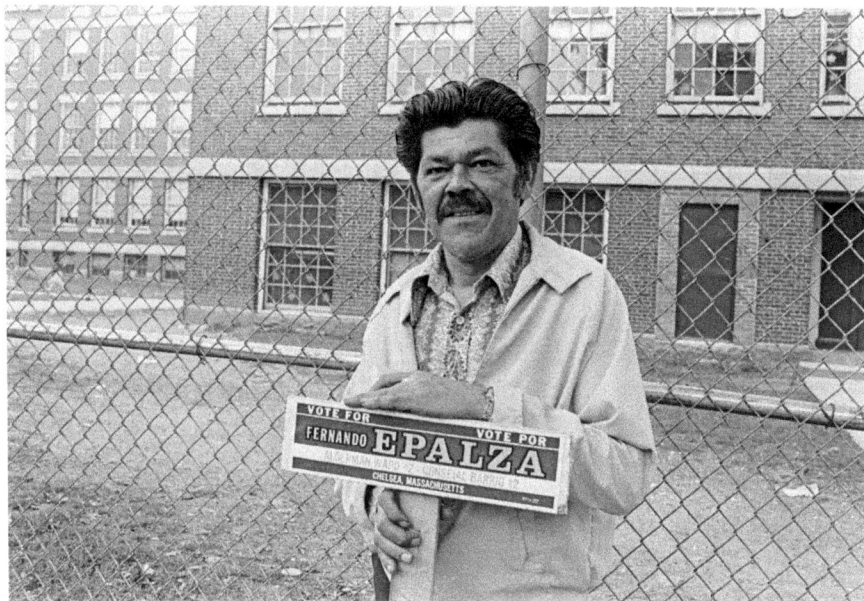

Canvasser for Ward 2 alderman candidate Fernando Epalza.

office free space for their ideas, their animosities and their complaints in black and white on tree pulp.

The 1977 mayoral election was our introduction to Chelsea politics in all its lavish, exquisite vulgarity. A young lawyer, Alderman Joel Pressman, was running for mayor against an older city hall type, Alderman Tom Mace. In the parlance of this day and era, Alderman Richie Clayman took delight in describing this race as "the Jew versus the Irishman." Very few serving in public office or working inside Chelsea City Hall or living in the city's five wards could disagree with Clayman's blunt description.

The quiet, unassuming Mace was a working-class type who came from Mill Hill, the Irish neighborhood on the northern edge of Chelsea on the Revere line, separated from that city by the edge of the Chelsea Creek (where the ice skating rink is today). His father, also named Tom, was one of the most popular people in the city when Chelsea was a far different place than when Arnie and I arrived. The elder Tom Mace won election time and again as the alderman from Mill Hill. It was natural and expected that his son should take his place.

Joel Pressman's father had been a state representative from Chelsea and a lawyer like his son, who followed in his father's political footsteps. Pressman

Right: Tom Mace for Mayor, 1977.

Below: Joel Pressman on election night, declaring victory over his opponent Tom Mace, by a margin of six votes, 1977.

Mayor Joel Pressman at his desk at city hall, 1978.

grew up in a two-family yellow brick home on Shurtleff Street, in Ward 2, where his late father kept a law office. Pressman, in his late thirties, beat Mace, in his late forties, by only six votes in the 1977 mayoral election.

When Pressman was coming up, we all believed he would be the savior of the city: the bright-eyed, bushy-tailed Jewish lawyer rising to save the city from itself. Like the young JFK, a bust of whom Pressman kept on his desk at city hall, we all believed in his promise. When Pressman beat Mace by six votes, Pressman supporters were relieved to know the city's future would move forward unimpeded. Nothing expressed was about freedom. It was about compulsion.

Some notable events marked Pressman's six years as mayor. Most visibly, he changed the face of Broadway, the main commercial corridor bisecting Chelsea. He brought in new, Victorian-era lighting, coordinated signage and laid new brick sidewalks and manhole covers, bronze sculptures cemented into them. He also created "Chelsea Walk," an alleyway between a barroom and a pizza shop that featured large photographic posters mounted on steel panels depicting the history of the city. This charming addition to an

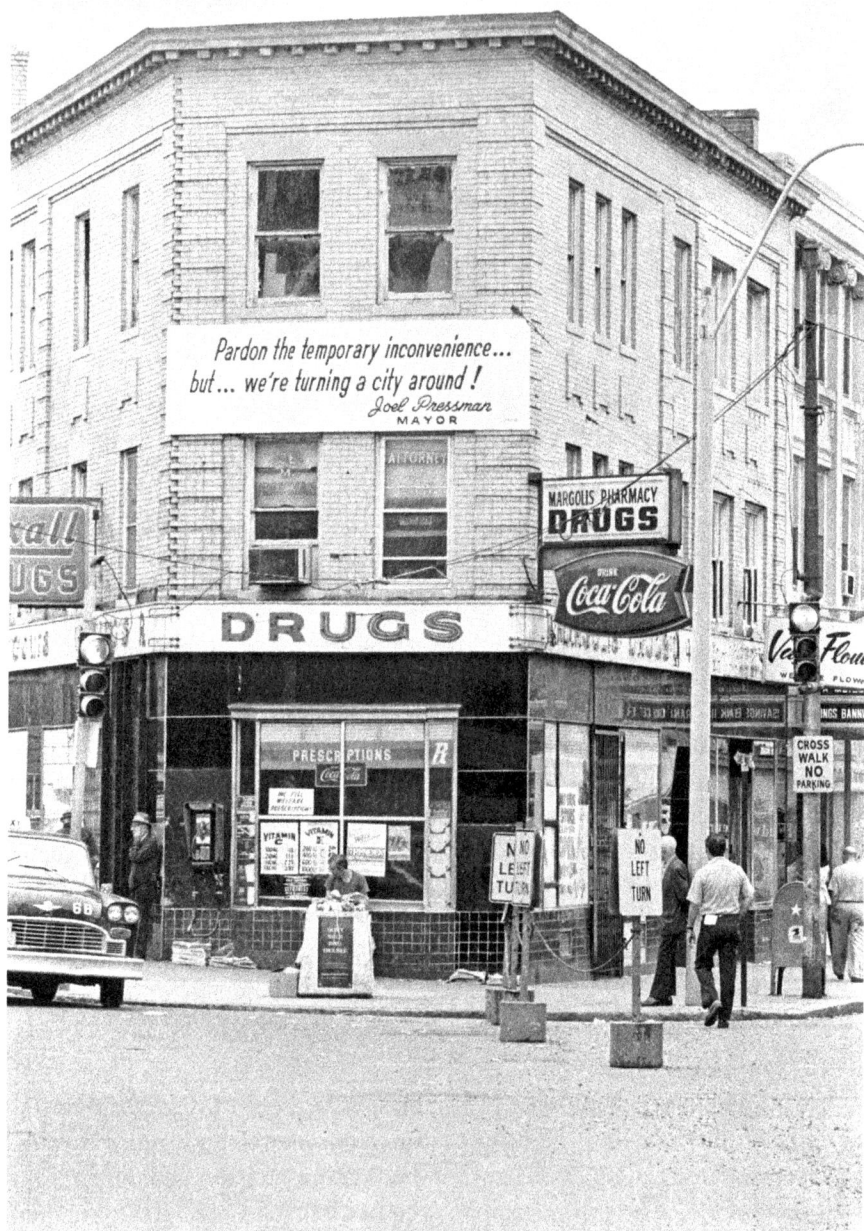

Pardon the Temporary Inconvenience, 1977.

Police Chief Abraham Burgin
presenting the city government, 1980.

otherwise unchanged Broadway failed to turn around either the reputation
or the direction in which the city was heading.

Pressman's most notable achievement was the transformation of the
former Naval Hospital site along the Mystic River, which had been closed
since 1975, into Admiral's Hill, an upscale housing project of eight hundred
new units for the upwardly mobile who came into the city. These newcomers
bought the brick-front townhouses and apartment condominiums on
a landscaped hill at a steep discount. It is still the closest thing to a gated
community in Chelsea, and the development supports itself, taking care of
all its own responsibilities, including a private security detail.

However, the downsides outweigh the upsides of Pressman's three terms.
The city suffered the loss of three major manufacturers: Sweetheart Paper,
which supplied McDonald's; American Biltrite Rubber, which moved to
Mississippi for the lower tax rate and cost of doing business; and Cabot
Paint, the city's most distinguished producer of paints, lacquers and stains—
also the city's oldest, most reliable polluter of the Chelsea Creek. Cabot
moved to New Hampshire into an environmentally sound property. The

loss of these three major employers, representing about two thousand manufacturing jobs, made city hall Chelsea's largest employer—and that spelled big trouble for the local economy.

Pressman didn't discontinue the tradition of allowing widespread gambling throughout the city sanctioned by him and given a green light by the police chief and his vice squad, all of whom were paid to allow illegal gambling in Chelsea. Of all the unethical mayors before and after him, Pressman was the most corrupt. "You didn't only have to pay once to get a permit," recalled a developer. "You had to pay twice!" Whether it was a liquor license, a bar license or a mall OK, whatever was up for renewal or a needed a permit or other approvals from city hall, it had to be paid for during the Pressman era.

While touring the city in our automobiles, Arnie with his camera and I with my reporter's notepad, we almost always ended up near the last house on Third Street. This house was Harry German's ancestral home—the last remaining three-decker in that utterly empty and barren stretch of open space left by the devastating 1973 Chelsea Fire. That open space, perhaps twenty acres, was like a barren moonscape. Just seventy years before, this

Jup the Clown at Chelsea Summer Expression event, City Hall Plaza, 1981. One of Joel Pressman's achievements as mayor was to organize these popular cultural entertainment events in the summer.

Last house on Third Street, 1979. After a drawn-out stalemate, the city exercised eminent domain to raze Harry German's ancestral home and build a shopping mall on this land in Ward 2 destroyed by the Great Chelsea Fire of 1973.

trash-strewn, vacant space with a decrepit three-family home at its center was the city's hub of immigrant life and commerce. That lonely three-decker stood like a single tombstone to remind us of what came before. Arnie's photograph of Harry German's homestead depicts that broken-down wreck, built right after the first Chelsea fire in 1908, as a monument to nearly everything that had befallen this place called Chelsea. If there is a historical masterpiece in this volume, it is this image of that last house and three trees that had miraculously survived the 1973 fire, with the photographer's shadow lengthening in the late afternoon light on the frozen earth of that abandoned site.

A new mall, anchored by the Kmart and a half-dozen smaller clothing stores and other shops, was planned for this site in Ward 2, once the most populated part of the city but now totally depopulated. The planning for the mall took a great deal of public debate at city hall by the board of aldermen. But the most difficult negotiations took place in private between the mayor and the owners and the builders of the mall. The difficult negotiations required kickbacks and bribes paid by the developers to the mayor.

The consensus among Chelsea residents about the new mall was that it was going to fail. People had difficulty believing anything positive could change the decline of the city into nothingness. They were right about the mall. After a short run of about six years, the mall went vacant and sat there as empty and lifeless as a cemetery. It became an albatross. Not until the Market Basket supermarket chain bought the mall and developed it in the mid-2000s did it achieve full status as an economic building block in the city.

Pressman served as mayor for three terms, from 1977 to 1983, when he stepped down to become the head of the Massachusetts Industrial Accident Board. Pressman announced he was leaving city hall for a job at the statehouse in Boston. But just days before he was to start this job, Pressman was arrested. A 1995 superior court criminal investigation into crime and corruption in Chelsea revealed his underhanded dealings under the pretext of saving the city. He was indicted, tried and ultimately disbarred for perjury and bribery for certain of his activities while mayor of Chelsea. He was forever disgraced. In a final act of ignominy for one of Chelsea's favorite sons from an esteemed family, Pressman moved to Revere.

Joel Pressman came to embody everything that would bring Chelsea down a decade later: from accepting payments, bribes and kickbacks for redeveloping land in Ward 2 razed by the 1973 fire into a shopping mall, to excluding the growing Hispanic population from government and in general making a mockery of the honest administration of the city government. He let us all down.

In the annals of Chelsea political history, no election for mayor can compare to the battle between Jim Mitchell and Tom Nolan in 1983. Mitchell and Nolan fought all summer long in a tight race. The city was split. Both of them ran spirited campaigns. Mitchell said he was going to free city hall from Mr. Quigley's influence, and that of the *Chelsea Record*, as well as from the old line who didn't want him to become mayor. He told Arnie and me in public meetings we covered, "You're not from Chelsea. Go back to Marblehead where you belong." He didn't care for the two Davids (Probation officer David Greenspan and Tax Assessor David Newman) or for Police Chief Charlie Wilson and the aged Jewish city treasurer Sydney Brown.

Tom Nolan was backed by Mr. Quigley, the *Chelsea Record* and the old-line leadership at city hall. Nolan promised a smooth transition to a better time with everyone remaining in their positions. He promised seamlessness at city hall.

Tom Nolan on the roof of a car in front of city hall, 1982.

Mitchell said he was going to clean house. He was going return power to the people. He was going to reduce the *Chelsea Record* to irrelevance and take down Quigley while he was at it. He hated Mr. Quigley. He was a combative controversial type, an outspoken politician. Ironically, much of Mitchell's prior professional life was spent at the *Chelsea Record* as an advertising sales manager.

During the last week of the campaign, Nolan got in a bar fight at the Beacon Café on Beacon Street, which Arnie and I owned then. After exchanging harsh words, our bartender, John Bohill, punched Nolan in the head by the bridge of his nose. This was the end of his campaign to defeat Jim Mitchell. Nolan suffered a black eye. He didn't go around campaigning in public for almost the whole week before the election. He lost by a razor-thin margin. "This proves there are more of them than there are of us," Mr. Quigley said to me, referencing Mitchell's rise to power and the change of direction in the city's political winds. Mr. Quigley never got over Nolan losing the race because he got punched in the face inside our bar. Neither could Arnie and I toss to the side the fact that Nolan's candidacy, which had been winning, was lost inside our bar.

On the night of the Mitchell victory, groups of Mitchell supporters shouted and screamed as they marched and marauded up and down Broadway and adjacent city streets, tearing down Nolan signs and assaulting Nolan supporters. It was as if we were in a zombie movie, skirting danger everywhere we went. It was probably a bit more reminiscent of wild crowds attacking one another during the chaos caused by the French Revolution in Paris.

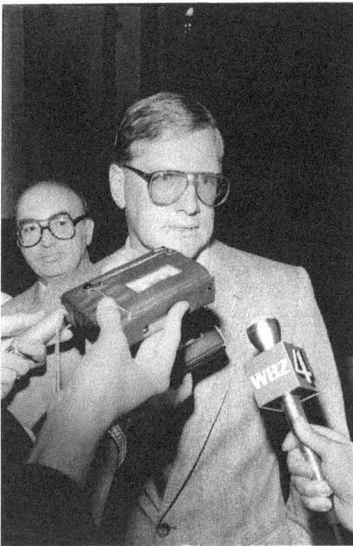

Mayor Jim Mitchell, 1984.

At the Irish Club, Arnie and I were jostled and tossed from the club, physically removed. "Get out of here, you bastards," a Chelsea firefighter and ally of the mayor shouted at us. "You aren't welcome here." Later on, at the *Chelsea Record*, all of us lamented the new day dawning in Chelsea. "So much for magnanimity in victory and magnanimity in defeat," Mr. Quigley told us. Thus began the Mitchell era at Chelsea City Hall.

When Jim Mitchell took office in 1983, he fulfilled a lifelong dream of becoming the mayor of Chelsea. Some people fight to succeed, and some people fight to fail. Mitchell fit the latter designation. By the summer of 1984, a recall effort to remove Mitchell from office was well underway. More than three thousand signatures had been collected in the recall led by Timmy McBride, a Harvard-educated Chelsea guy. His mother, Elizabeth, was a member of the Chelsea School Committee. His father had owned a small liquor store on Cross Street.

The mayoral recall committee had 3,000 signatures out of a needed 3,232. What was the problem? Mitchell disappeared from his office at city hall. He stopped coming in shortly after taking the oath of office in June 1984. On July 3, he reappeared. In rapid succession, Mitchell suspended the police chief and the city treasurer, sending five police officers to city hall to have him removed. "I'm going to be the mayor forever," he told reporters. Six weeks before, he said he was going to resign. Mitchell vowed to beat the recall. "I will be mayor this term and the term after that." He announced the suspensions at an early morning news conference at city hall. Only local reporters were allowed to be there. I was in attendance.

When Alice Wilson, eighty-one, found out her son had been suspended by the mayor, she put a gun inside her handbag and made her way to city hall. It was crowded with residents, Mitchell supporters and recall supporters when Mrs. Wilson came in. She was going to confront Mitchell. She started up the marble stairs leading to the mayor's office where Mitchell had barricaded himself, refusing to speak with the media. Halfway up the staircase Mrs. Wilson collapsed, setting off a wave of hysteria.

After his press conference, Mitchell harangued two reporters: Howie Carr of WNEV-TV (Channel 7), who had earlier reported Mitchell saying he was going to resign, and me. Earlier in the day, Carr and I had camped out on the front porch of Mitchell's home in Prattville. Mitchell came out of his house and threatened to physically toss Carr and me from the porch. We left and went down to city hall. At the news conference, Mitchell said Carr was a "first class phony" and "slime" and I was a "Howie Carr clone." His behavior early in the day and as the day wore on became of concern. He appeared to be unraveling.

The tension at city hall crested as Mrs. Wilson was taken from the stairs on a stretcher and rushed to the Whidden Memorial Hospital in Everett, where it was reported she had suffered a heart attack. A short while later, Mitchell sent a police officer to escort the city treasurer from his office. That effort was headed off at the pass by city solicitor Evan Geller and longtime city clerk Johnny Dalis. In another twist, the officer sent to remove Brown was Sergeant Phil Spellman, a former mayor. Spellman did not remove Brown. Geller and Dalis said that because the mayor had not hired Brown (the aldermen hired him, technically), he could not be suspended by the mayor. This didn't deter Mitchell. He announced he was going to fire another sergeant and a police officer.

The crowd milling about inside city hall dispersed after a bomb threat around 4:00 p.m. Firefighters searched the building. No bombs were found. Alderman Stephen Powers, the owner of a sub shop in Mill Hill, demanded Mitchell's resignation that night at a standing-room-only hearing at city hall. The aldermanic chamber was packed with noisy opponents of the mayor. Powers blocked Mitchell from speaking. "This is the last time he's going to make a mockery of this board and a mockery of this city," he said to the large crowd, which cheered him wildly. "He's lost complete control of the city," Powers added. More wild applause and cheering erupted inside the chamber.

Councilor Stan Triosi, a prominent voice in the city's Italian community, called it "a sad day." He said the suspensions constituted the beginning of a reign of terror by Mitchell. I thought Mitchell was showing that he was unbalanced. Watching his actions, a lot of people felt the same way. His flushed red cheeks and his tendency to lock himself inside his office were unsettling.

After the hearing, Mitchell told a *Boston Globe* reporter, "There's no way the recall petition is going to succeed." He was right. It didn't. So went the summer of 1984 in the life and times of Chelsea's political history.

A federal investigation into public corruption at Chelsea City Hall began in 1992. This led to Mayor Butch Brennen giving up the keys of the city to Governor William Weld, who threw the city into receivership. The game was finally over. The public corruption that plagued the place and its politics for almost a century had finally come to an end. At that moment in Boston at the statehouse when Mayor Brennen stood with Governor Weld while a dozen television cameras rolled, the city couldn't pay its teachers and was going to be forced to close the public schools. The payroll for police and firefighters could not be met, and city workers were going to go unpaid. The city treasury was empty. Chelsea had hit rock bottom.

In the ensuing months, the federal investigation into public corruption in Chelsea indicted former mayors Tom Nolan, Jim Mitchell and John "Butch" Brennen. They were all tried and convicted of accepting bribes

Mayor Butch Brennan dedicating Harry Nyman Square, 1989.

and kickbacks and for lying before the grand jury. They all served one form or another of home arrest or jail time.

Six police officers were also ensnared in the investigation, including the former vice squad chief, referred to by Mr. Quigley as the "Chief of Vice." Captain Buddy McHatton received a one-year term for tax evasion. Several of the officers served jail terms; they lost their jobs and their pensions. All of them were proven to have been paid by Chelsea's gangster king Sammy Berkowitz for allowing illegal gambling in the city. Former mayor Joel Pressman, as part of the investigation, was also indicted for accepting money to facilitate the building of the Kmart Mall, which led to his disbarment.

Under the receivership, Chelsea lost its right to elect a mayor ever again. The city charter provided for a new city manager form of government and a vastly reduced set of powers for the board of aldermen, limited to one power, voting for the city manager's contract. Everything about politics changed. It remains the same today, almost thirty years after receivership.

3

A PHOTOGRAPHIC ESSAY OF PEOPLE AND PLACES

The impression forces itself upon one that men measure themselves by false standards, that everyone seeks power, success, riches for himself and admires others who attain them while under-valuing the truly precious things in life.
—*Sigmund Freud*, Civilization and Its Discontents

The opportunity to photograph Chelsea was truly a gift given to me. I am thankful to the people of this city who supported and embraced my work every day at the Chelsea Record.
—*Arnie Jarmak*

Arnie Jarmak's compelling, and at times, stunningly candid, portraits of Chelsea's men and women, the old and the young, living out their lives on the street, the sidewalks in front of their homes, parks and places of worship, reveal the truest, tragic "face" of the city during this era. The portraits are masterful images embalmed inside a moment brought to life with this book. The closeups Arnie took four decades ago are telling glimpses into their subject's lives. They are the updated urban equivalents of Dorothea Lange's and Walker Evans' WPA records of 1930s Great Depression-era poverty. Arnie's portraits depict the difficult, hard and—at times and in certain places—impossible lives these people led throughout this small city.

Besides Arnie, the only other photographer who lived in Chelsea during this time was Harry Siegel, an itinerant portrait photographer who most days could be found on the corner of Broadway and Fourth Street. Harry would take your picture for twenty-five cents. He used a primitive box camera mounted on a tripod and developed your photo right there on the spot. His hands and fingers were discolored from working the negative with chemicals inside the box. He placed the small finished image in a decorative cardboard frame with sayings at the top like "Forever Yours." He was one of the most visible and well-known street people in the city. Everyone we knew had their photo taken by Harry Siegel at least once or twice during this era. He memorialized our presence in Chelsea in the group portraits he took of me, Arnie and Andrew Quigley (see page 44).
—*Joshua Resnek*

Cottage Street couple, Ward 3.

Harry Siegel, Chelsea's own itinerant commercial street photographer.

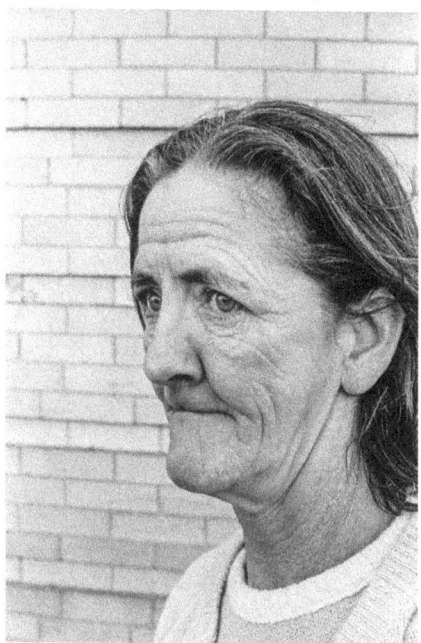

Clockwise from top left: Woman on Marlborough Street; Man in derby hat; Man in cap, Bellingham Square; Woman on Fourth Street.

Allen's Cut Rate, Broadway.

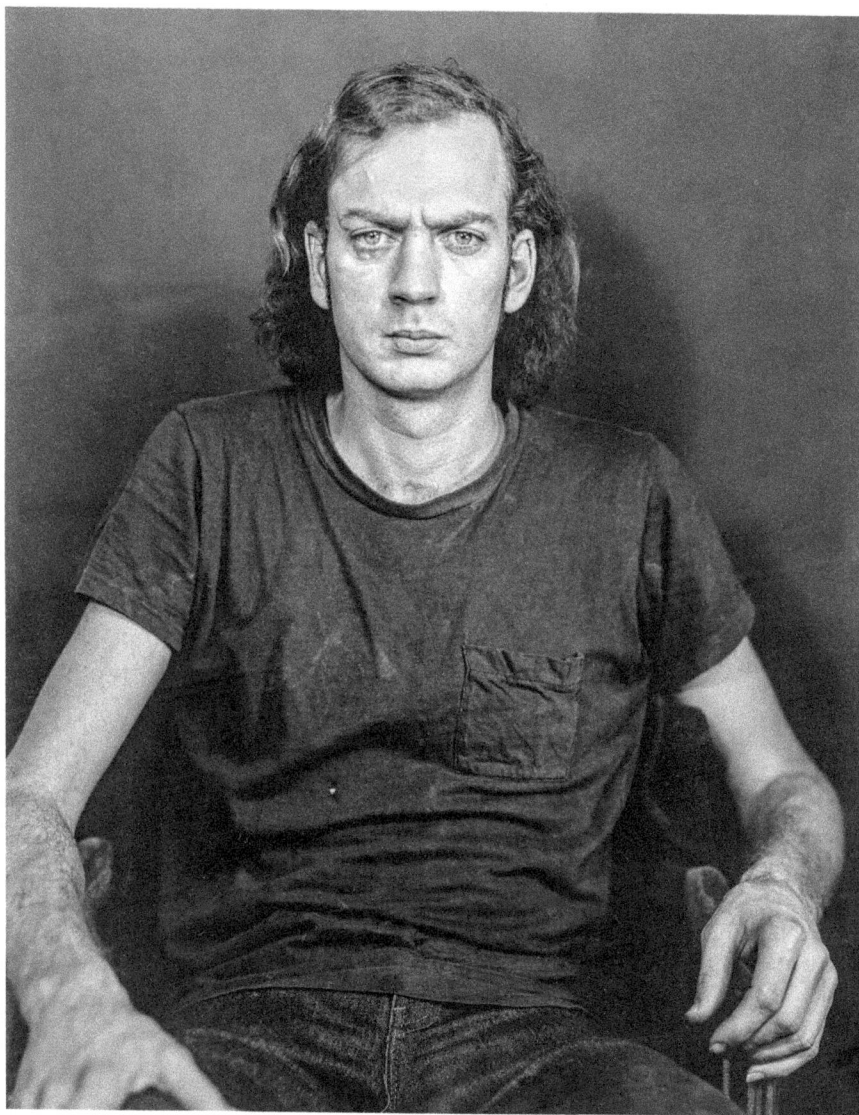

Steve, Lower Broadway, Ward 2.

Clockwise from top left: Lieutenant, Engine 5, 1981; Andrew Quigley Jr., 1982; Young girl at night; Man on Broadway after the 1978 blizzard.

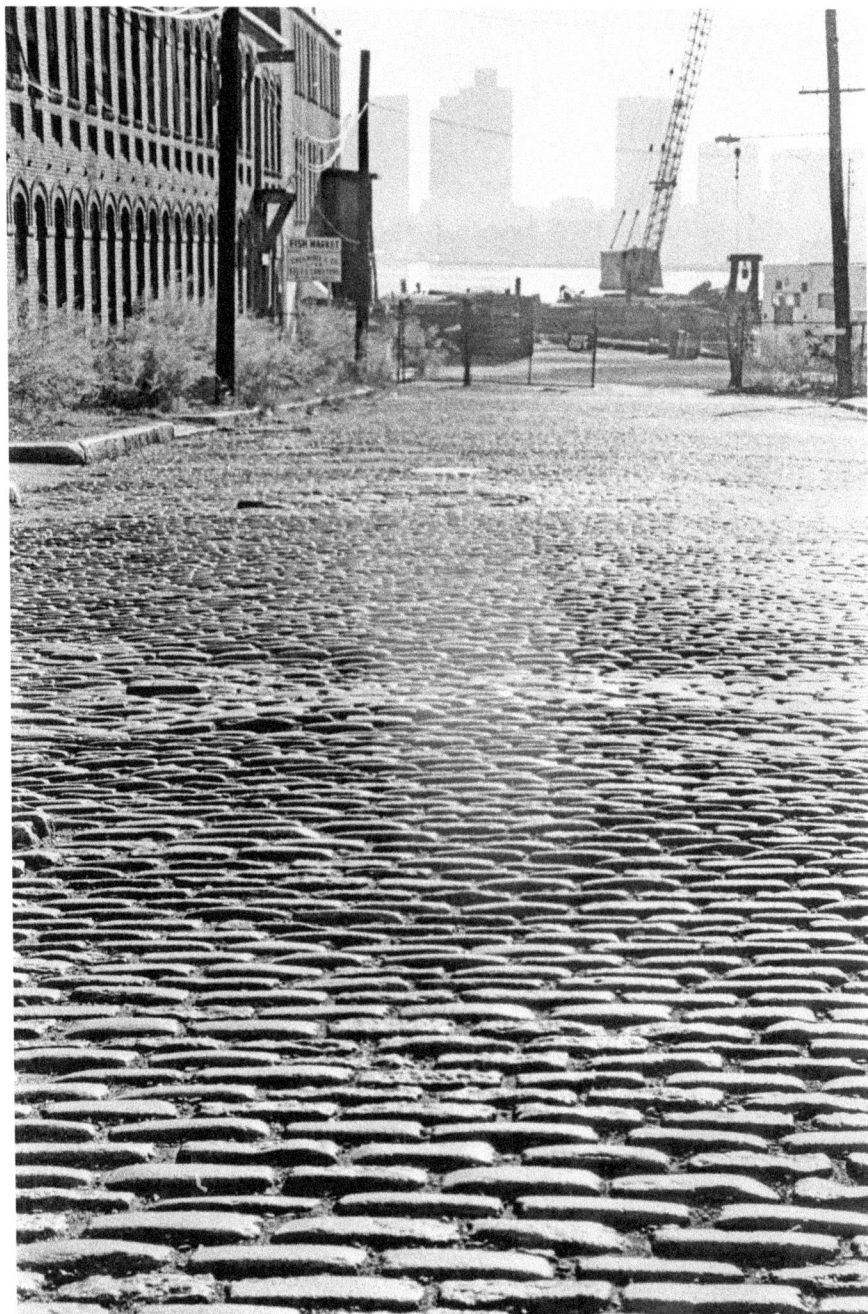

Winisimmet Street, Ward 2. This is one of the last remaining cobblestone streets in Chelsea and leads to the Mystic River; Abraham Lincoln arrived to speak in Chelsea in 1848 via a now long-gone dock that was here.

Man pondering life in Bellingham Square.

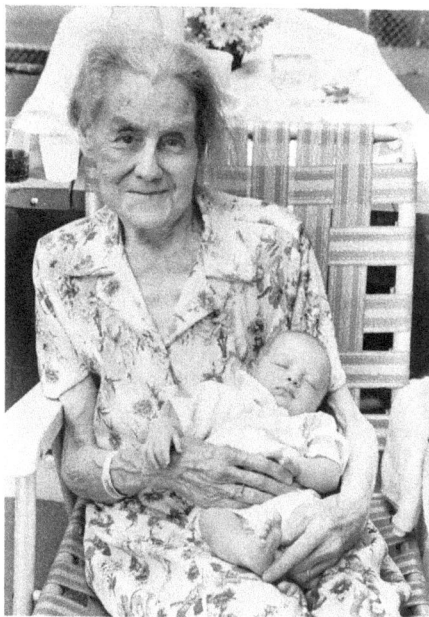

Left: Little Girl in Polonia Park.

Right: Cycle of life, Ward 3.

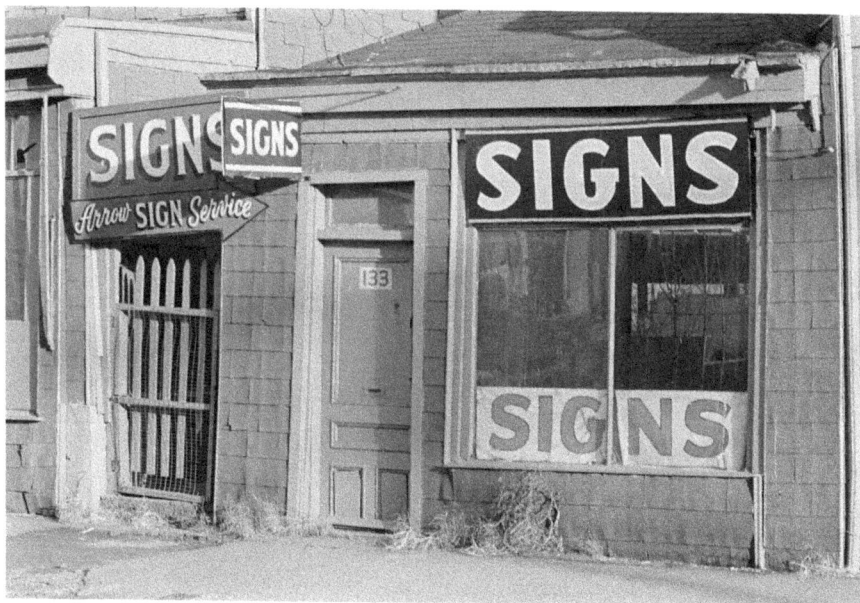

Arrow Sign Service, Ward 1.

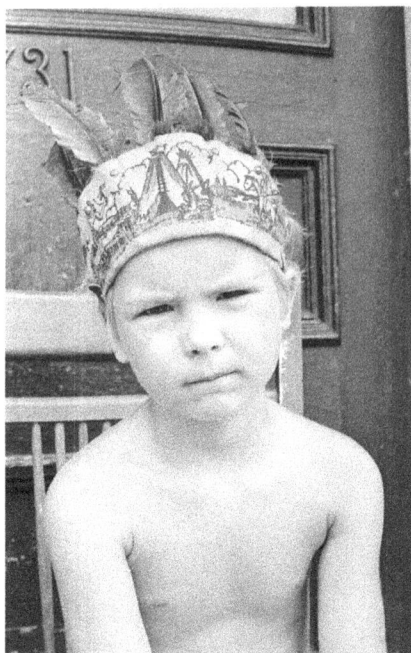

Above, left: Richy.

Above, right: Cowboys and Indians, Ward 2.

Left: Benny Keith in the 1978 blizzard.

Knights of Columbus, Chelsea Square.

Clockwise from top left: Man in Bellingham Square; Miss Fitzgerald; Living on the edge; God Made the Irish #1.

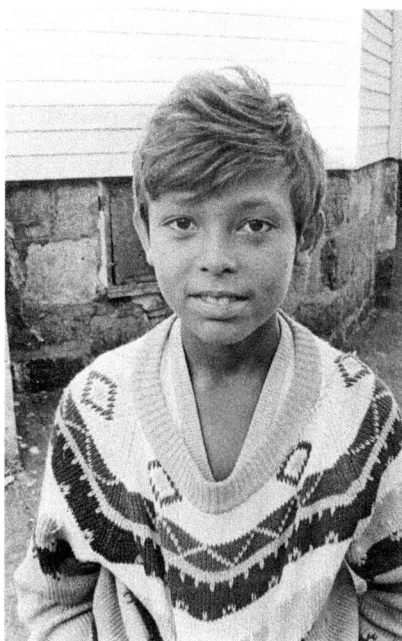

Left: Shurtleff St. school kid.

Right: Hand-me-down sweater, Ward 1.

Kids and sofa.

Left: Memorial Day, Garden Cemetery.

Below: Edwina, one month before her death in a fire.

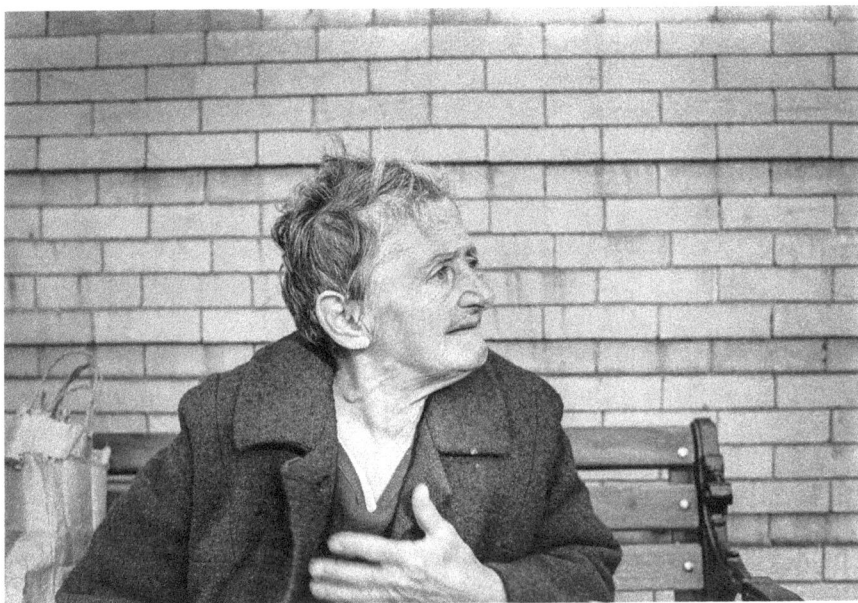

Doris Popejoy, New Year's Eve.

Broadway couple.

Young couple at Chelsea Walk, off Broadway.

Young love, Bellingham Square.

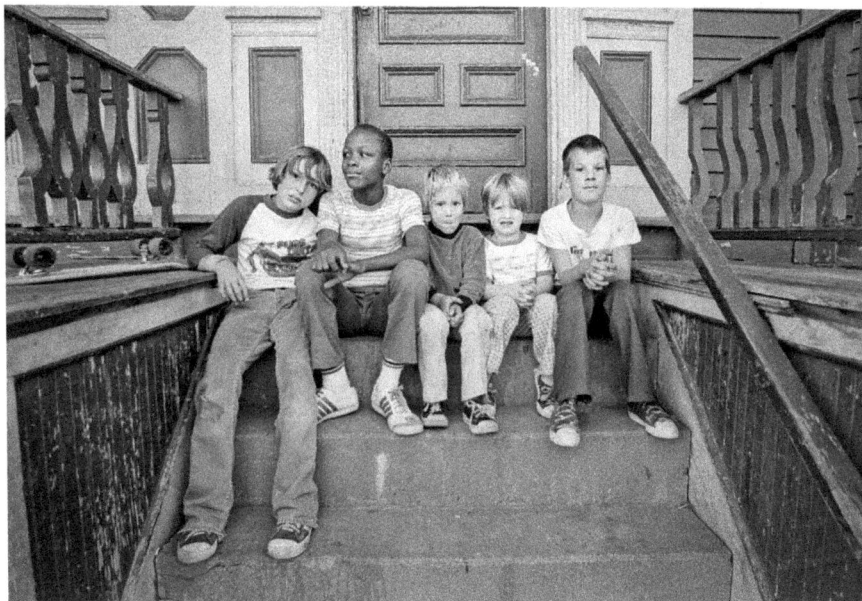

Five kids sitting on a stoop, Ward 1.

Kids on a porch, Ward 4.

First Communion.

Above: Six kids standing on their building stoop.

Right: He Men.

Lady on sidewalk.

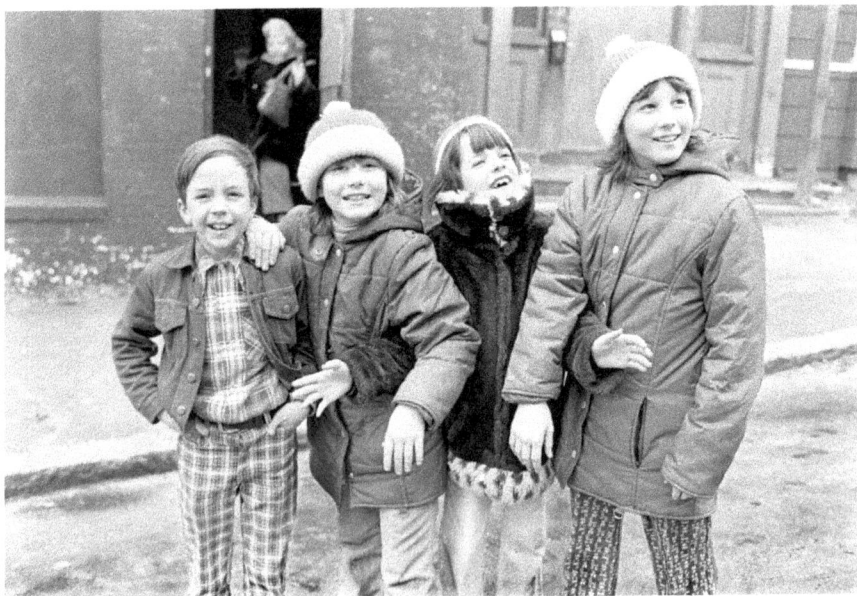

Playing in the streets of Ward 2.

Chelsea Clock Fire, 1980.

Top: Claire in the Studio.

Bottom: Girl at Bosson Playground.

4

ENVIRONMENTAL INSOLVENCY

In the summer of 1983, Arnie and I ran from time to time to Revere Beach from our three-family stucco house at the end of Pembroke Street in the waterfront district. We ran long distances daily during this era of our lives. We ran five, ten or twelve miles every day; on some days, we ran the ten miles each way to Marblehead. This run in July 1983 was a historical Chelsea run of sorts for us, our first to Revere Beach. Until Chelsea became a city in 1857, Chelsea owned Revere Beach and neighboring Winthrop. "It was all one big place at one time," as Mr. Quigley would often say. We could feel Chelsea at Revere Beach.

We were in great physical condition during the years of turbulence, but the city where we lived was not. The residents of the city and its political leadership had long ago abandoned preventive care for survival, for getting by instead of moving forward, for putting up with everything befalling them, instead of fighting back or reinvesting. The major industrial polluters remained untouched by Chelsea City Hall. The state had little or nothing to do with them. The Chelsea environment gestated—unhealthy, dark and dreary.

The outflow of thousands of middle-class families, and of capital, and the dereliction of the city's housing stock, coupled with the influx of some of the poorest immigrants to arrive in the city, all contributed to the darkness enveloping the place as we found it when we arrived.

We purchased a building on Pembroke Street, a short street just off the thoroughfare of Williams Street, in 1978 for $9,000 and lived there. Looking

View from Pembroke Street rooftop looking southeast toward downtown Boston.

back, it seems almost unimaginable that this much real estate, just a mile from downtown Boston, could be purchased for $9,000 then. Over the years, property in Chelsea devalued. Land values declined. The environment imploded. We could have bought every three-family home on the street for $150,000—and we did just that over time.

Our home served as a metaphor for nearly all the multifamily housing stock in the city when we got there. Nothing meaningful had been done to improve properties on Pembroke Street since their construction in the 1890s. Our three-family was pretty much the way it was when it was built in 1898 when we settled into the second floor.

The second floor we lived in did not have central heat and was not insulated. We heated the place with a wood stove and with what was known as a gas-on-gas stove—a cooking stove with a gas heating element—that actually kept the small space comfortable at 60 degrees for us—uncomfortable for nearly anyone else. The windows rattled in their rotted casements when a breeze blew off the river. In the deep cold of winter, the place was almost unfit for habitation. Original brass plumbing plagued the place. The electrical wiring was unfit for modern usage. Plugging in an air conditioner would likely have burned the place down.

Pembroke Street, Beacon Street and Medford Street, Chelsea's poor equivalent of the brownstones on Beacon Hill in Boston, were untouched by the Chelsea fire of 1908, but nearly every building perhaps one hundred yards away went up in flames and smoke during that April conflagration. In fact, since the Roaring Twenties, when the city achieved the zenith of its growth as a typical American industrial and residential melting pot city, very little new construction had taken place.

The Great Depression nearly killed the city. Chelsea's economy sank with that of the nation but at a far quicker pace into a much deeper social, economic and political abyss. From the onset of the Depression until the election of Dwight Eisenhower as president in 1952, nothing had been done but a seasonal sweeping of the streets or perhaps a repair of broken water pipes, installed after the Great Fire of 1908. With the exception of Prattville, the housing stock resembled a giant, undifferentiated slum—from street to street and ward to ward.

In the early 1950s, the opening of the Mystic River Bridge (now called the Tobin Bridge), connecting Chelsea with Charlestown and points north, marked the splitting of the city in two. The giant steel riveted structure was painted green with a lead-based paint. The roadway, which came to be known as the Expressway, an extension of the bridge, traveled a long, straight line through the heart of the city, cutting its streets in two and, over time, becoming the city's worst polluter. Air quality suffered every day from the toxic exhaust wafting from heavy car and truck traffic moving on the Expressway and crossing the bridge. The air became fouled. Chelsea's air quality was among the worst in the state and has remained this way into the present.

By the late 1960s, the lead paint covering the steel trestles of the Mystic River Bridge and the Expressway began corroding and chipping, the chips falling like snowflakes. When the bridge was repainted for the first time, workers sanded and scraped massive amounts of lead paint-soaked chips—which fell on the houses and land below. These were the days before painting companies were required to work in enclosed spaces, with the workers wearing protective gear.

A generation of kids growing up near the bridge in Chelsea played in tiny yards or front lawns saturated with lead paint chips. Many of the youngest children unknowingly ate the chips of lead paint, or the paint got into their cuts while playing in yards or small playgrounds covered in bits of paint. Many residents with small gardens ate lead-tainted vegetables grown in lead-saturated earth. (Ingesting lead paint has been shown to have a disastrous

Left: Tobin Bridge from Admiral's Hill.

Below: Marginal Street tank farms with Tobin Bridge in the distance.

effect on learning and brain development in children.) By 1970, Chelsea's children living near the bridge and the Expressway had the highest level of lead paint poisoning in the United States.

Chelsea's reputation for poisoning its children was considered to be of epidemic proportion in some environmental and medical circles. Lead paint was found in nearly every apartment in the city, as it had been used without concern for its possible health hazards. In a city where poverty ruled and life was tough, kids inside these lead paint-infested apartments ate small chips or got it all over themselves and were poisoned. During the turbulent years, laws became more stringent. Apartments had to be de-leaded before they could be rented, but for many Chelsea kids, lead paint poisoning ruined their lives.

Water quality was poor; the city's river, its creek and the waters of the Mystic River were polluted. Oil tanks lined the Chelsea River from the end of Broadway to the beginnings of Chelsea Creek, where the public ice-skating rink stands today. Oil leakage over the decades seeped downward to the water table, destroying whatever natural water quality existed. Seepage from those tanks polluted the land under them and all around them. The entire Chelsea shoreline and the land adjacent to it was polluted.

Our residence on Pembroke Street had a cemented backyard. It sat at the end of a row of four nineteenth-century red brick buildings. Next door, a large, one-story, cement block refrigerated structure painted white was used by Kayem Foods to manufacture hot dogs.

The only other living thing on Pembroke Street besides us and the other residents was a hardy one-hundred-year-old Italian grape vine that blossomed every summer and ran up the rear of our home like a giant snake. In the basement of our home, the original Italian builder had constructed a grape crusher to harvest the grapes and bottle his own red wine. When we took over the property, that vine had grown thick and strong, climbing three stories up the back of the house. When in full blossom, the grapes extended in abundant purple clusters all the way from the cemented backyard to the top of the house, growing in and around a wooden support system the original builder erected over the second and third floor rear doors.

When we arrived in Chelsea in 1977, there was not a stitch of grass or a blooming flower on Pembroke Street nor on any of the streets that ran parallel to it down to the shore of the Mystic River. Wherever raw earth once existed, it had been cemented shut from the sun and the elements since before we were born.

Chelsea Creek marshlands around Admiral's Hill.

The Mystic River was almost hopelessly polluted. It was so dark and dense that algae couldn't grow. Some of the Vietnamese who moved to Chelsea about the same time we did fished the river for food to feed their families from the Meridian Street Bridge separating Chelsea from East Boston at the mouth of the Chelsea River. Swimming in the Mystic River was bad, but swimming in the Chelsea Creek was worse. They were both health hazards.

Sewage up and down the creek had been pouring into the river for two centuries when we arrived. What drained from the various manufacturers lining the creek from the waterfront residential district to the Forbes Industrial Park about one and a half miles away? The world-famous Cabot Stain and Paint Company had been pouring a huge volume of disinfectant, wood preservatives, shingle stain and iron-reducing materials from outfall pipes directly into the Chelsea Creek since the company set up shop in Chelsea in 1882.

The nearby American Biltrite manufacturing plant didn't pollute the water so much as it polluted the land along Marginal Street, affecting the ten-acre site and everyone living in multifamily row housing surrounding it, especially on Maverick Street down to Highland Avenue. Biltrite manufactured rubber and hosing, shoe heels and a plethora of rubber products. The entire neighborhood stank of rubber and chemical residue day and night. If you worked inside the plant, you also stank when you got let out of work to go home.

The shipbuilding industry polluted the shore itself from the 1860s until it disappeared in the early part of the twentieth century. All that remained of it

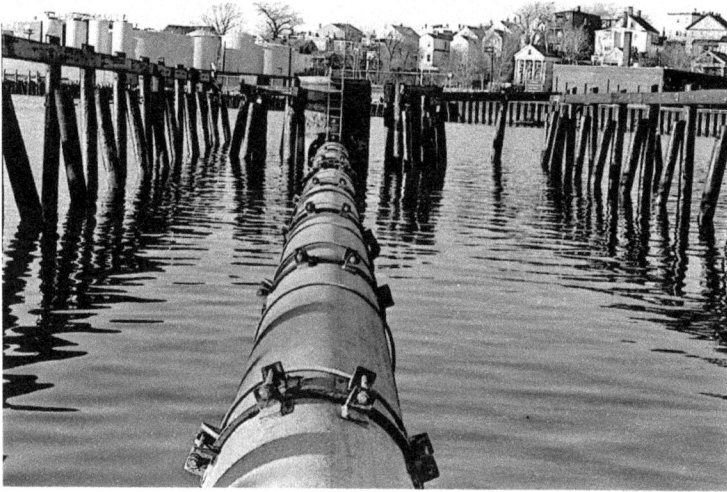

Sewage overflow pipe exiting into the Mystic River.

when we arrived were the timbers and pilings that supported the industry—decades of wood tossed into the creek where it soaked and then rotted out.

Noise pollution from nearby Logan Airport at seemingly every hour of every day added to sleep deprivation for many and made others just plain angry. In those days, all incoming flights always used a route over Chelsea that came in so low you could see the landing gear with the naked eye. The constant noise pollution drowned out conversations and made life miserable for those trying to sleep at night and was yet another imposition on living a sedate life minding one's own business in the city of Chelsea. Finally, in 1989, Logan Airport officials implemented a new plan for dispersing the noise and air pollution to the nine communities surrounding the airport by installing new runways and alternating the flight paths.

All of this taken into consideration, we believed our three-family stucco building facing Boston to be a great find, and frankly, it was an incredible place to live at the start of our time in Chelsea. There was a romance to the place and especially to its positioning.

Above all, Chelsea's location, with its proximity to, yet isolation from, Boston, its own colonial history dating to 1624 and its indigenous history dating to much earlier, gave it a perverse kind of Shangri-La character. As James Hilton describes in his 1933 fictional masterpiece *Lost Horizon*, Shangri-La is a sacred, hidden place of refuge, an earthly paradise where the residents are immortal, living in a permanently happy and hidden land isolated from the world. Club Chelsea was dirty, tired, decrepit and old, with many of its elderly living lives of quiet desperation. Yet we found life in Chelsea, for all its deficiencies and inequities, more vital than the

129

Texaco Gas tanker, Chelsea Creek.

pristine suburbs we grew up in. Chelsea had ocean views, high hills and an undulating surface. Tired housing—much of it Victorian—made for many, many charming spaces with sunlight and detail for people to find a space for themselves for a fraction of what it cost to live in Boston.

From the roof of our $9,000 three-family building on the Chelsea waterfront, unobstructed views of the rising Boston skyline just one mile away to the east stared back at us brilliantly. On a sunny day in the spring or the summer, young men's and women's dreams about their lives got uplifted beyond any of the exigencies of seemingly being stuck in Chelsea, looking out at the world from the tops of roofs all over the small, struggling city. The prevailing breeze off the water soothed the soul. It charged our creative spirit. We were at the top of the world, at the top of our world.

We began our run to Revere Beach heading down Williams Street, passing onto Marginal Street, then meeting the Revere Beach Parkway and running along the Chelsea Creek until the road turned toward Revere Beach. At the beach, we began what was usually our daily run to the Point of Pines at Eliot Circle, turning around and then running back to Chelsea on the same route.

On this day in July 1983, the temperature had soared into the nineties. When we made it back to the Meridian Street Bridge, running on trash-strewn paths along the edge of the Chelsea Creek (also known as Snake River), we took off our running shoes and shirts and jumped into Chelsea Creek. We swam for perhaps forty-five minutes, out to the center of the creek, luxuriating in the freedom of so daring a jump into so polluted a river. We got out just as an oceangoing oil tanker, directed by tugboats, slipped into its berth at the Gulf facility on the East Boston side of the small river. We didn't get sick and we didn't die from swimming in the polluted water, but when we returned to nearby Pembroke Street, we took hot showers to wash away a veneer of crud.

Although historical records of swims in Chelsea Creek are not kept, it is quite likely we were the first two men to swim out to the center of the river in a half century. It is also quite likely that no one has swum out to the center as we did in the last forty years. After our swim and showers, we went up to the roof, sat in our chairs and looked out at our world. It was a stunning view, an easy place to dream and to re-create in our minds what had come before Man so altered the environment in the name of progress and profits.

Several hundred yards away from our Pembroke Street rooftop was the former Naval Hospital, empty and boarded up, at the top of what is now

Swimming in the Chelsea Creek off Clinton Street bridge.

known as Admiral's Hill. The hospital opened in the early 1800s and closed in 1975; it was one of the few large empty sites in Chelsea that was not contaminated, though it was directly adjacent to the Tobin Bridge.

During 1980–81, developers brought in by Mayor Joel Pressman, then in his last year as mayor, created a residential community of brick-fronted townhouse condominiums angling all over the Naval Hospital Hill. A huge public park buffered the townhouses from the Mystic River. The Admiral's Hill development was led by the distinguished architect Robert Verrier, a man with vision who felt the heartbeat of Chelsea's soul. For the first time in its modern history, Chelsea residents had access to the waterfront.

The Sagamore Indians had been hunting ducks and geese living on this land for at least five hundred years when Samuel Maverick (circa 1602–circa 1670) came from England in 1624 and put up a palisades hut on this hill, known now as Admiral's Hill. Maverick, and a tiny band of others who arrived in a trickle for the first few years, did a daring, carefully choreographed dance that brought them closer together to the Sagamore as a new age dawned in North America.

In the Chelsea we moved into, a few lonely misplaced ducks, geese and robins might be spotted here and there, but the majority of fowl in the area were pigeons and seagulls. Virtually no fish lived in the Mystic River, and the Chelsea Creek was piled with trash. At low tide, it presented quite an eyesore. At high tide, the full flush of the Atlantic filled creeks and tributaries, inundating low-lying areas, and the swampland turned into a dockage for boats in front of the casino resort just over the border in Everett today.

Maverick's account of living on this land is full of death-defying twists and turns, in spite of the land being absolutely untouched. According to Wikipedia, in March 1635 Maverick sold his holdings outside his farm in Winnisimett to Richard Bellingham, the deputy governor of Massachusetts. The parallels between the colonial and modern eras, in learning how to overcome life's difficulties, are instructive. For the new white settlers, survival from day to day during the winter was a fight to remain warm, to eat, to eke out for themselves the existence the Sagamore had mastered over the centuries. The new community of white, Protestant English settlers growing along the shore of what came to be called the Mystic River became friends with the Indians. They traded together. They hunted together. They came closer out of necessity brought on by a shortage of food supplies during cruel, early winters or summers without rain that caused crops to fail.

Waterfront, looking toward Marginal Street.

Maverick and the Sagamore, from their perch on Admiral's Hill and in the marshlands and tidal flats a short walking distance west—where the casino resort has arisen quickly—looked out on a pristine, wondrously natural world abundant with fish and game, beaver and deer. It was a veritable Garden of Eden—unspoiled by the hands of any man. From the roof of our building on Pembroke Street, very near to this exact spot, we looked out on a thoroughly modern world completely stripped of its relationship to this untouched past. We had to shut our eyes and hold our noses in order to dream about what existed right here before Man "improved" the land.

SEND-OFF

From 1980 until the collapse of the city in 1991, Chelsea residents drew glimpses here and there of the future. During the period between 1980 and 1987, for the first time since the Roaring Twenties, the value of Chelsea's properties began to rise. For a short time, it appeared as though a tremendous rise was in the making. Some of us could feel the speculation. New people were coming to the city. The power to create motivations pushed so many baby boomers into a new reality. Chelsea came alive, for just a bit.

Arnie and I bought the Beacon Café, Chelsea's oldest bar, on Lower Broadway in the shadow of the Tobin Bridge. We bought it in 1982, at the same time the city seemed to be rising, and owned it for nine years. For a while, the success of the Beacon served as a perfect metaphor for the short upward swing the city experienced. We changed the Beacon Café from a biker hangout into the city's most popular bar and restaurant. The Beacon rocked and rolled during this heyday era. It was arguably the nicest bar in the city, with punched tin ceilings, brass railings, checkered tablecloths, Hunter fans, a fifty-foot-long polished mahogany bar and a clientele that mixed old Chelsea with the new.

From 1982 until 1987, the Beacon was crowded every night. The new trade we had attracted—businessmen and residents, some Admiral's Hill residents, young people trying to find one another in their lives—drank side-by-side with old-timers and longtime Chelsea folks. It was the one place in the city where the new Chelsea felt comfortable mixing with the old

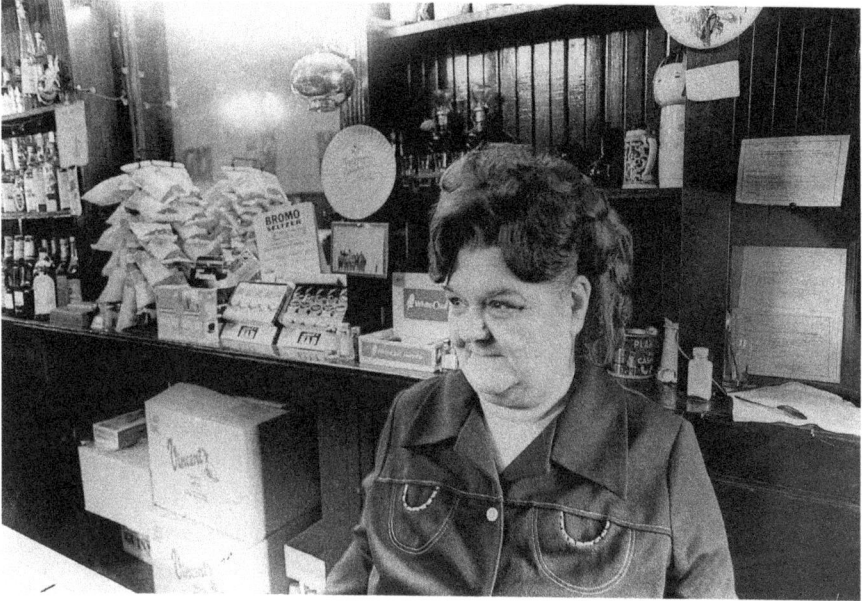

Helen at the Beacon Café.

Chelsea. The Wednesday night before Thanksgiving became a tradition for a decade for Chelsea High School graduates returning home for the holiday from college. By 1987, the business was beginning to fall off. By 1989, it was failing. The party scene had burned itself out. The Go Go 1980s were coming to a close—even in Chelsea. We closed the Beacon in 1991. Others understood the beginning of the rally was the moment to buy—and that five years later would have been the moment to sell.

Many properties doubled and tripled in value, especially multifamily residential apartment houses. The per-unit price for a property rose from about $3,000 when we got to Chelsea in 1977 to about $25,000 by 1986. Our little stucco three-family we bought for $9,000 would have sold for $75,000 to $100,000 in 1986. The prices were rising because Boston had grown so expensive during this period. Developers driven out of Boston began speculating side by side with the locals. More than a handful of younger developers and owners led by Matt Simon and E.J. Ahern, Richie Clayman and Richard Voke and James D'Amico felt comfortable in Chelsea and, what's more, found that the city liked them.

D'Amico occupied a space of his own, that of the largest owner of residential housing in the city, probably eight hundred units. One of the best-known people in the city, D'Amico, in his early forties, drove around the city in a white van filled with glass, door bolts, locks and light bulbs, toilet plungers and pipe dope—answering calls to the various tenants requesting something from him. The image of him in his pressed khakis and clean work boots was that of a wealthy Chelsea businessman, one of the wealthiest in the city, working every day on his properties as a repairman. Jimmy never sold when prices rose. He never sold when prices fell. He picked up his rents from his nearly all Hispanic tenancy. Most of D'Amico's tenants loved him. D'Amico owned about seventy properties. Not one of them was ever marked with graffiti.

Speculation in the real estate marketplace caused everything to value upward. New people were coming into the city to invest in Chelsea and to live in the city—because the city had a spark and seemed an exciting place to be for the more adventurous who could not afford a neighborhood like Jamaica Plain. I called the newcomers urban pioneers: yuppies, mostly white, and educated. At the same time, many of the Chelsea old-timers and those from old Chelsea families hanging on saw no hope for a return to what had been. Nothing new under the sun pleased them. These new people coming into the city were not a cause for joy. For many of the hangers-on, the newcomers were intruders into their disappearing society. The city would be better without them, many of them thought.

The newcomers' view of Chelsea was overtly, almost vehemently, apolitical. The new folks took no interest in local elections or local politics. City hall was just another nameless, faceless building for many of the newcomers. They tended not to care about the mayor, public corruption or decadence, payoffs, bribes and the full litany of Chelsea's municipal crime system in all its incarnations. Chelsea, for the new wave of younger people walking down Broadway, shopping in small shops in Cary Square, walking their pets on top of Powderhorn Hill or eating in any number of pizza places and sandwich shops spread around the city, was a new and exciting experience. There was street life on Broadway, traffic everywhere, lots of smaller stores and owners wanting to talk with you about who you were and what you were about—who came to know you. Coming into Chelsea was all about discovery. After all, for forty-five years, no one wanted to come to Chelsea to live. Newcomers reveled in pushing back against that wall. Very few people living in the Chelsea of this era lacked a sense of self-importance about telling others where they came from whenever asked.

"I'm from Chelsea," they'd answer affirmatively with a bit of an emphasis to shatter any doubts about the authenticity of their comment. Who outside of the city could imagine anyone wanting to say they are from

School committee chairman Andrew Quigley addresses the graduating class at Chelsea High School Memorial Stadium.

Chelsea, let alone being proud of coming from Chelsea, and understanding intuitively what it means to grow up in a place like this and to take it out with you into the world. What a thing that is—don't underestimate its power. This is what gave, and what continues to give, Chelsea its grandeur and its underclass glory.

The outside came inside during these years when the city government was spiraling out of control. Reporters from Chicago and Los Angeles interviewed Mr. Quigley at the *Chelsea Record* when he was acclaimed for bringing Boston University in to run the city's bankrupt public school system. It was the first instance of the privatization of a public school system in the nation's history. As chairman of the school committee, Quigley was instrumental in persuading BU's President Dr. John Silber to have the university take over the public schools. The university immediately made available twelve full scholarships for high-achieving Chelsea High schoolers. BU turned around the image and the reality of the public schools.

New energy, new direction, new leadership and enormous amounts of private money were injected into the public schools, which had been hobbled by more than 60 percent of the student body being nonnative English speakers and even illiterate in their own language (Spanish, for the most part). Chelsea reading scores were and still are ranked among the lowest for public schools in Massachusetts—but nowadays that is not because of a lack of funding. Yet some Chelsea High School–educated kids got accepted to Harvard, Yale, Brown and other fine schools, and many more were accepted to four-year colleges all over the nation.

A powerful sense of pride in the Chelsea community prevailed. Mr. Quigley's keynote high school graduation speech was a highlight for the graduates and for all of us participating in the life and times of this small city. My sons, Jacob and Joseph Resnek, both graduated from the Chelsea Public Schools. Jacob went on to University of Massachusetts. Joe graduated from Harvard and Harvard Law School. As Jews and Anglos, they were a minority of two at a Chelsea High School serving mostly Spanish-speaking kids but also kids speaking a dozen other languages from all over the world. My son's childhood friends, none of whom were white or Jewish, all have college degrees. To a person, they are proud to say, "I come from Chelsea." What a thing to hear and bear witness to. In their minds, their badge of honor is coming from Chelsea, growing powerful in their lives because of their special upbringing in so small a place during such a difficult time. For them, coming from Chelsea made them a life force, a pedigree that would serve them well when they entered the world

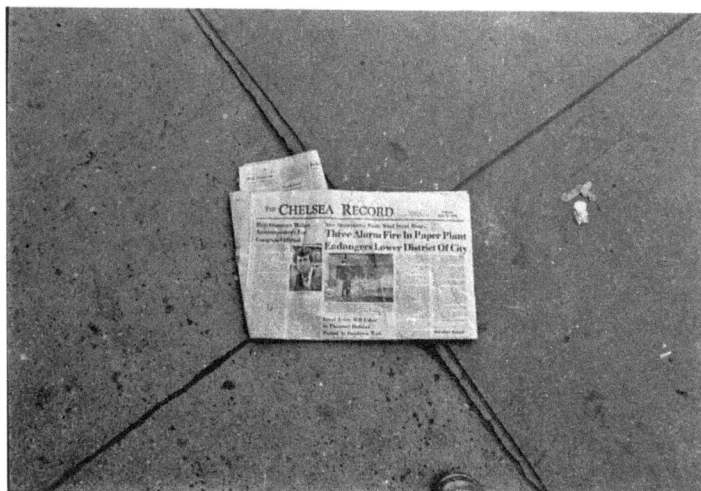

Copy of the *Chelsea Record* on the sidewalk.

and mingled with the wolves. Despite the violence, the indifference to poverty, the pollution and the poor housing stock most of them all grew up in, they succeeded. Most of them moved out of the city. Most of them could recognize a 14-karat fraud one hundred feet away—and they were rarely scared. It's hard to scare a Chelsea kid.

In 1989, Boston University awarded an honorary doctorate to Mr. Quigley for his role in privatizing Chelsea's public schools. When Mr. Quigley was called by an official from Boston University who told him about the planned honor, he said he was caught off guard, he recalled. "Are you sure you have the right Quigley?" he asked the caller. "Are you *sure* you have the right Andrew Quigley?" It was quite an honor for the *Chelsea Record* publisher, Chelsea resident and chairman of the Chelsea School Committee to be recognized in this way by a major university.

During the great years of real estate speculation in Chelsea, many of us prospered. Arnie and I bought and sold properties. Others bought to hold. Others overpaid, buying at the wrong time of the cycle. The rotted underpinnings of the city were crumbling. All the years of theft and ineptitude were winding down to an anticlimactic end. When the IRS real estate tax laws changed in 1988, everything started going the other way again and with greater vigor. A severe recession was on the way. Development didn't just stop in Chelsea. It slowed down and stopped nearly everywhere.

During the latter part of the turbulent era, the Young Men's Hebrew Association closed down. No more daily camaraderie with people from all walks of life coming in to what used to be a synagogue to play basketball or to lift weights. No more steam baths and sunning oneself in the afternoon at the one place that epitomized Club Chelsea. It was a time when old city institutions were failing and closing, disappearing just like that, with the snap of a finger. The Elks Club closed and moved to Saugus, as if you can have a Chelsea Lodge Elks that is located miles away. The Walnut Street Synagogue and Temple Emmanuel were the last two remaining synagogues in a city that once boasted twenty-five of them.

At the end of this great run, Mr. Quigley sold the *Chelsea Record* to a publishing group from Revere. They moved the office to Revere, where it remains today. The new ownership did not have much interest in Chelsea. We were both fired.

At the end of the turbulent years, the last elected mayor of Chelsea, John "Butch" Brennan, was indicted for municipal corruption, as were former mayors Tom Nolan, Jim Mitchell and Joel Pressman. As the court findings rose out of a federal investigation into public corruption in Chelsea that had begun in 1990, three out of the four former mayors served prison sentences or time under house arrest.

When Chelsea couldn't meet the payroll for its schoolteachers and other public employees in 1991, Mayor Brennan threw up his hands. He said it was over. He called Governor William Weld. They talked. One of the major welfare cities in the commonwealth was now entirely on state welfare. Elections were suspended. Contracts, too. Political haggling ended. The governor put the city into receivership.

That afternoon, I drove Brennan to the statehouse to hand over "the keys" to Chelsea to the State of Massachusetts. I drove the last elected mayor of Chelsea on the final day he would serve over the Tobin Bridge to the statehouse in my car. He was reflective. He seemed relieved. How fitting for a *Chelsea Record* reporter to witness the last moments of the last mayor of Chelsea. The governor appointed James Carlin to lead as city manager and free it of its corrupt and inept politics, its doomed financial policies and chaos that had taken it down to its knees.

A FBI investigation extended beyond former mayors Nolan, Mitchell and Pressman. It led to the retirement, the firing or the imprisonment of five Chelsea police officers, including the chief of the vice squad, Captain Buddy McHatton. McHatton served time for tax evasion. The four other officers were indicted for aiding Chelsea's King of Crime, Sammy Berkowitz, in one way or another in return for favors or cash payments.

The upward swing we experienced in Chelsea as two men in our late twenties was followed by a calamitous end in the early 1990s. We were heading in another direction by the time we hit forty. The end of our youthful heydays and a particularly colorful era in Chelsea came at great personal cost to many investors and Chelsea homeowners, including me. After a few brief years of light, Chelsea property owners returned to their prison cells. The real estate market tanked—much deeper and faster than in Boston. The urban pioneers left first. The developers went broke or were unable to sell their properties for what they put into them. The city changed. Chelsea was again heading into the ground. Arnie and I head into the ground with it.

In 1992, I appeared on *Sixty Minutes* with Mike Wallace, who interviewed me about the Chelsea experience. Wallace's piece was titled "Chelsea on the Rocks." The two-camera shoot took place inside the law office I was living in after losing all my money and working as an investigative reporter. This was shortly after the city went broke. When you're working as an investigator, you are mostly broke. When you're broke, you recognize generosity, or the lack of it, more acutely.

A new generation of street people and the walking wounded of American society replaced the old-timers who were dying out. New faces came out of Bellingham Square's sorry rooming houses. The drug addicts seated on benches in front of the post office zoned out. Most of those waiting for the bus into Boston on the corner of Fifth Street and Broadway wished it would come sooner. Broadway's major stores like Gorin's and Hy's had closed. They were replaced by smaller stores featuring Vietnamese foods and goods or Hispanic stores selling Goya products. Clothing stores served the Hispanic community. The old white man's haberdashery was gone.

A host of the characters we knew left the earth during this time. The venerable street photographer Harry Siegel, the old vaudeville actor Benny Keith (always appearing like he was walking out of a 1920s stage act), the dapper Jimmy Lawlor, the insurance man from one of Chelsea's oldest Irish families still walking around in spats, all died. Pickles Nyman, the Quigley ally who drove around Chelsea delivering laundry with Quigley signs on his station wagon, died. Sam Pressman died. The two Davids—David Newman and David Greenspan—died. All their deaths were noted by me in the *Chelsea Record*.

I wrote many obituaries during these years of tumult. I memorialized the well-known and the unknown, the rich and the poor. I wrote a front-page John Lennon obituary. I wrote an Elvis Presley obituary. I wrote my father's obituary. I wrote obituaries for war heroes—guys and gals—who served in the armed forces during the World Wars, Korea and Vietnam. I wrote obits for the street people and the mayors, the public officials and the geriatrics who were just trying to hang on. I sent these Chelsea personalities off, as Mr. Quigley would refer to it. I even wrote Mr. Quigley's send-off.

The send-off was important to Mr. Quigley. It became important to me. History meant something to both of us. He believed strongly in sending-off the mighty and the meek, the rich and the poor, the Jews and the Irish— and everyone else. I listened to him deliver many eulogies, using his golden tongue, first, to overpower and, second, to bury his political opponents (most of whom attended all the same funerals) with powerful, literary, Irish orations. He always sought to touch the collective heart and soul and to persuade many to think the eulogy was better, more entertaining and intelligent than the person for whom it was delivered. Mr. Quigley was a Pericles in disguise.

Mr. Quigley's death came at about the same time as my father's, and together, their deaths closed this era of my life. Chelsea wasn't the same without the Quig. He was our greatest supporter. He was very generous to us. He gave us jobs and living quarters, and he taught us what loyalty is. The Quig liked a good fight. Above all, he published our work. He taught us how to conduct a battle. He understood the rules of engagement—when to advance, when to pull back, when to attack with all your might. "You treat your friends like friends, Josh," he would say to me. "And you treat your enemies like enemies."

Mr. Quigley was a master of self-deprecation. In all the time I was by his side, I never heard him boast or make fun of a political opponent by name. He was generous. He didn't like others paying for him. When he appeared at a local wake, he always went to the back of line, chuckling a bit to himself, watching the mayor of Chelsea and other high officials cut to the front of the line. He liked being in control. He had patience. He never acted overtly when he was attacked for his politics or the paper was condemned because of what he wrote. He always waited before acting. He gave out more than he received as a politician. He received great praise from residents as the writer of a locally acclaimed column "Short and Sweet." He knew how to tell a tale. His column was often the talk of the city. Still, in the year before he died, he talked to me about his life and his sense of unfulfilled promise. Everything about this extraordinary era ended with Mr. Quigley's burial at Woodlawn Cemetery in Everett in 1990.

For Arnie and me, glory as young men was working as journalists and being published in the *Chelsea Record* every day. It couldn't get any better than this, at that time, for us. When we look back at these years spent in Chelsea with Mr. Quigley, his sons, Stephen and Andrew, the rest of the staff, and all the friends we made throughout the city, they are the greatest years of our lives. How lucky we were to have worked for Mr. Quigley.

ACKNOWLEDGEMENTS

WE WISH TO THANK our image curator, editor and longtime Chelsea resident Amy Ingrid Schlegel for guiding us in shaping the manuscript and with the all-important choice of photographs. Her strict attention to editorial correctness and detail as well as concern for aesthetics impressed us and was the positive influence we needed to bring this long-planned project to life. We are deeply grateful for her willingness to take on this key role and for her friendship.

JOHN KENNARD'S EFFORTS TO correct and perfect the original 35mm and 8 x 10 negatives for publication was an act of true artistry and love. The digital perfection of the photographic imagery throughout this book is largely due to his unyielding efforts and diligence as both a superb technician and a photographer in his own right. We thank him for his commitment and for his professionalism.

WE ALSO WISH TO thank Elias Polchiera for lending his expertise and artistry to the preparation of many of the 35mm negatives as digital images.

ABOUT THE AUTHORS

Arnold "Arnie" Jarmak is a documentary photographer and entrepreneur. He founded Jarmak Corp. in 1998 and reclaims antique lumber from New England's defunct mills and repurposes them for commercial and institutional clients. Raised in Marblehead, Massachusetts, he has been based in Chelsea since 1977. Jarmak's favorite book is Thorstein Veblen's *Theory of the Leisure Class*.

Joshua Resnek is a newspaper publisher and editor as well as independent investigative journalist based in Boston's North Shore. A native of Marblehead, Massachusetts, he was based in Chelsea from 1977 to 1991 and then from 1991 to 2012 and was a part owner of the *Chelsea Record*. He is currently the publisher and editor in chief of the *Everett Leader Herald*. Resnek's favorite book is Tolstoy's *War and Peace*.

Jarmak and Resnek met in the first grade and have been friends and colleagues ever since.